CASINO

Dave Shaw was born in Wolverhampton but now lives in Nuneaton. He works for Peugeot and nurses a life-long ambition to write professionally.

Aside from Northern Soul, Dave's other passions in life are his seven-year-old Mitchel – who he is sure will become a "Soul Boy" of the future – and Wolverhampton Wanderers, who, one day, Dave hopes to see play in the Premier League.

Casino is Dave's first book, and is the culmination of his twenty-five years on the Northern Soul scene, as well as the fulfilment of a long cherished dream. Although the work took five years to complete, it was twenty-years in the planning stage.

To Ian

Best wishes

CASINO

DAVE SHAW

Dave Shaw

BEE COOL PUBLISHING (BCP) LIMITED
Published by Bee Cool Publishing (BCP) Limited
PO Box 16924, London SW18 4ZU
First published 2000
Copyright © Dave Shaw/Bee Cool Publishing Ltd 2000

Printed and bound in Great Britain by Butler & Tanner, Frome, Somerset

A CIP catalogue record for this book is available from the British Library

ISBN 0 9536626 2 4

Thanks to Russ Winstanley for permission to reproduce the *Northern Noise* article on page 115

"Going To A Go-Go" Words and music by Rogers Robert, William Robinson, Marvin Tarplin & Warren Moore
©1965 Jobete Music Co Inc, USA
Reproduced by permission of Jobete Music Co Inc/EMI Music Publishing Ltd, London WC2H 0EA

Every effort has been made to contact copyright holders for their permission to reprint material in this book. The publishers would be grateful to hear from any copyright holder who is not here acknowledged and will undertake to rectify any errors or omissions in future editions of this book.

For Penny Fisher and Phil Shelton

ACKNOWLEDGEMENTS

THE FOLLOWING PEOPLE deserve more than mere thanks, they deserve a lifetime of gratitude; their help in writing this book is just the tip of the iceberg.

THE FRIENDS

Keith (Mr Wags to you, guy!) Henry – the straightest thing to come out of West Bromwich since the M6, remember, "When tha's tripe on t'cow pat, tha's nowt wrong wi' owt." Thank you brother.

Paul (Harpo) Harpin – we've come a long way since the car park of the Ashmore, mate: Rotherham, Blackburn, Peterborough, Stafford... Wherever we end up next, I know you'll be the same old 'scunston'. Times, guy. Good times.

Ian (Gamber) Clayton – anniversary tickets? No problem, chap! Let's hope the Wolves finally get promoted, mate...If they put you and me in charge we'd get the job done in four hours! See you in the Hatherton before the play-off final!

Elaine Soley – the blonde bombshell from Kiddy! Thanks, 'Laine, for everything you've ever done for me, and everything you never did. I'll always 'luv ya'.

Colin (Atlas) Humphries – author of the immortal lines: "Well it ain't no joke, we're the lads from Stoke: Bob, Geoff and me, we're the famous three..." The guy with the best footwork of any dancer I've ever seen. Atlas! Here a minute...Alright, mate?

Gillian (Gabby) Balfour – perhaps it was too much too soon. "Di Wedi Mopio", you said. You did, Gabs. You really did. Be happy.

Caroline (Cleo) Thake – "Oh, you should see what I can see, when I'm cleanin' windows..." It was me that ended up with the broken legs, guy.

Estelle Finney – a shoulder for everyone to cry on. You were too good for any of us. I hope you find what you've always deserved.

And to all at Peugeot – here it is at last.

Time and space prohibits me from mentioning the other thousand or so. To all of you, (you know who you are) keep the faith.

I would like to thank the following people, without whose kindness and patience this book would not have been possible:

THE DJs

Steve Whittle – never more than 'one of the lads', never less than a true friend.

Richard Searling – who shaped the scene with his records, and saved it with his dedication. The all-time number one Soul Spinner!

Soul Sam (Martin Barnfather) – the DJ who gave the Northern Soul scene more than just great music, he also gave us a conscience.

Pep (Ian Pereira) – for his expertise and his friendship over twenty years, and for his continued belief in our scene.

Russ Winstanley – for his kindness, generosity and help, for starting the whole thing off back in 1973, and for inspiring me to write.

Dave Evison, Brian Rae, Keith Minshull, Dave Thorley, John Vincent, Alan Rhodes, Ian Clark, Gary Rushbrooke, Pat Brady, Keb & Guy, Chris Plant and all the other DJs who have entertained soul lovers over the last twenty-five years.

SPECIAL THANKS

To Mike Ritson and Stuart Russell for making a dream come true; for their patience, their faith and friendship towards a total beginner!

And to my son Mitchel just for being there.

"COULD BECOME BIGGER THAN THE TORCH"
"AN INCREDIBLE ATMOSPHERE"
"BRILLIANT SOUNDS"

THE WIGAN CASINO
SOUL CLUB

CASINO

PREFACE

ON 19TH SEPTEMBER 1998, despite a vow never to return, I went home for the first time in almost seventeen years. That night, an all-nighter was held, at a club called Maxime's in the Lancashire town of Wigan, to celebrate the first-ever such event in the town. This had taken place a quarter of a century before in 1973.

Back then, the country was facing the prospect of a long, bleak winter with the advent of the 'three-day week' and the 'energy crisis'. Pay packets were lighter, and looked likely to remain so for some time, and an evening's TV viewing was usually cut short by a power-cut. Most people who remember 1973 do so with a grimace.

But something happened in September of that year which literally changed the lives of thousands of people, including me. At 2am on the Sunday morning of the 23rd, a decrepit, old dance hall opened its doors to around 500 youths and much to the alarm of certain sections of the town's populace and the local constabulary, remained open until 8am. The club had served the town of Wigan in many guises; as the Empress Ballroom, it was a focal point for the youth of the town during the war years, and later, it catered for a very different clientele as a snooker hall.

Finally, it had become the Casino Club under the ownership of local business man Gerry Marshall, and in this final incarnation it became not only the centre of the soul music scene in the UK, but also one of the most famous discos in the world: The Wigan Casino.

This book relates the most exciting, challenging and rewarding period of my life, when the Casino represented the halcyon days of Northern Soul.

My first visit to the club was not until 1975, when the biggest musical trends were glam rock and disco. Since then, we have seen the rise and fall of punk, jazz-funk, New Romantic, hip hop, house, and a multitude of others, yet Northern Soul venues still attract large crowds, and indeed, the scene as a whole is enjoying a boom in popularity on a par with those magical days of the mid-seventies.

I believe that Northern Soul will be around forever, because there will always be people who have more intelligence than to swallow the media-hyped garbage handed to them by the music moguls who have traditionally dictated the direction of popular music in this country.

Northern Soul is not just another music scene, any more then Otis Redding was just a singer. To its devotees, the scene is a way of life; an ideal to be defended at all costs. Those on the scene are a family, a community of like-minded people for whom soul is the only music. For me, and thousands of others, Wigan Casino was the ultimate experience; a time never to be forgotten, when the music of Black America was etched into our lives forever.

This was an era which has never been equalled, and will never be repeated. The music itself was what Wigan Casino was all about – the obscure soul music that originated in the ghettos of sixties Black America and kept the 'Heart of Soul' beating throughout the seventies and into the next decade.

The Casino experience meant different things to different people: there were those who loved to literally dance the night away; others more into collecting the original vinyl, and some who went simply to experience the club's unique atmosphere, friendship and camaraderie. But it was the music itself that unified us. A deep love for soul music and desire to 'Keep The Faith' – to make it last forever.

One of the best friends that I ever made at Wigan Casino was Keith 'Wagsy' Henry, someone who remains 'one of us' to this day. At a soul event some years ago, Wags and I were talking about the Casino (as we always do) and he said: "When you think back on all the things that we did back then, do you ever wonder if it really happened? I mean, could anything have really been that good? Or did we just dream it all?"

In my search for superlatives to describe what Wigan Casino meant to me, Wagsy's words beat them all hands down. So to the countless brothers and sisters I had the privilege to call friends at Wigan, I dedicate this book to you. I hope you find something that takes you back home to that crumbling old dance hall, the place that we used to call heaven. That alone would make all of this worthwhile.

To anyone reading this book with no knowledge or experience of Northern Soul and Wigan Casino, you have my genuine sympathy. Because in answer to my old mate Wagsy, yes, it did happen. And it really was that good.

Keep the faith.

DAVE SHAW

Part One
THE EARLY YEARS

*"Well there's a brand new place I've found,
where people come from miles around..."*

Chapter One GOING TO A GO-GO

1975. I WAS fourteen-years-old. My favourite artists, who I would defend to the point of violence, were the Stylistics, the Detroit Spinners, the Chi-Lites, the Delfonics and Barry White.

The glam rock scene was in full swing, and Slade, T. Rex and Mud were adored by my schoolmates. The previous year, a new era in mass-produced, commercial dance music had been born with the release of George McRae's "Rock Your Baby". All of the above had me reaching for the sick-bag.

As far as chart music was concerned, the only records that briefly caught my attention were Art Garfunkel's re-working of "I Only Have Eyes For You", a good smoocher for the end of parties, and Cockney Rebel's "Come Up And See Me" because my brother hated it.

As for the rest, Queen's "Bohemian Rhapsody" was, as far as I was concerned, equally as deserving of my ridicule as "Whispering Grass" by those two prats out of "It Ain't Half Hot Mum".

I was not being deliberately scornful of contemporary music; I was just another self-important fourteen-year-old amongst millions of others, needing a focus for his teenage rebellion phase – the one that comes between puberty and acne.

Dave McAleer, a long-time soul fan and A&R man for Pye Records, had been put in charge of the label's attempt to cash in on the trend towards the faster dance music being played in the clubs of Northern England. The records favoured by the dancers at these clubs, were mainly obscure, sixties recordings from small independent labels.

Pye raided its archives for similar soul material, and came up with a gold-mine of goodies from the vaults of sixties American labels like Scepter, Wand, Calla and Roulette, of which they owned the publishing rights. These labels featured a virtual 'Who's Who' as far as black soul artists from around 1963-1969 were concerned: Frankie & the Classicals, Jerry Williams, Maxine Brown and the Masqueraders all had material on the labels which was now at Pye's disposal. Thus was born the famous Disco Demand label, and with it, my twenty-three year love affair with Northern Soul.

One of these previously unreleased tracks was an instrumental 'Surf

Sound' by a Canadian band called the Chosen Few. The original track had a storming intro, an average middle and a shitty ending. McAleer took it into the studio and re-arranged it so that the intro was simply repeated throughout the song. The finished item was a striking, uptempo dance track, unlike anything else being played nationally at the time. For its UK release on Disco Demand, the name of the band was also changed to ally it to the dance trend up north. McAleer re-christened the artists after the town that was the centre of the fuss, and Wigan's Chosen Few was born.

"Footsee" made the top ten, selling over 180,000 copies. The new dance phenomenon took the country by storm, and Disco Demand's output soon repaid Pye's gamble with sales figures of over a quarter of a million copies, through reissues of obscure '60s discs that had largely been ignored in the US at the time of their original release.

Tradition dictated that the chart position of "Footsee" had also earned it a slot on *Top Of The Pops*, so McAleer recruited a troupe of the best dancers from Wigan's Casino Club, to show the nation the new dance craze. Ironically, my first introduction to Northern Soul, the music that ignored the conventional Radio One chart syndrome, was to be through *Top Of The Pops* and Tony Blackburn. I can see him now, all silk cravat and denim flares as he introduced the record to a breathless audience: "There's a new dance craze up north and it's sweeping the nation..."

I was captivated by the dancers; their footwork, acrobatics, spins and back-drops just blew me away, and I immediately vowed to give up Kung Fu forever and concentrate on my dancing career. Naturally, my thoughts were occupied with how to get to the Wigan Casino for one of its all-night sessions – now how was I going to manage that at fourteen-years of age?

I began to hang around with some of the older lads at my school who were 'into Northern', and from one lad, Steve Slater, who had already been to Wigan, came the ultimate accolade. One day in September, he told me that Wigan's second anniversary was coming up on the 27th, and that he had a spare ticket if I was interested. I was very interested indeed!

Persuading Mummy and Daddy to let me go was not as hard as I thought it would be, although I did lie about being offered a lift there and back in Steve's dad's car. When I think about it, it was a piss-poor piece of improvisation, and they probably saw right through it.

We had decided to hitch-hike to Wigan from junction 10 of the M6 motorway, not thinking how hard it might be, nor even caring about getting home safely, the only thing on our minds was getting there and being a part of it.

Saturday, 27th September 1975. Rain. Exactly what was not required for a two-hundred-mile round trip with only our thumbs for transport. Steve and I tagged on to another group of lads who were also hitching: four older members of the Wolverhampton 'Soul Set'; Phil Jordan, 'Chunky', John Caddick and Paul Walsh. Two hours later, all four had abandoned the idea, and gone back to Wolvo for the train, a luxury not open to us for financial reasons.

So we stood hunched against the rain and waited. And waited. By some miracle, at about 10.30pm, a Volkswagen Beetle stopped and the driver offered us a lift as far as Knutsford service station, where we managed to scrounge a ride with a coach from Gloucester. We were on our way.

An hour later, the coach pulled onto a huge car park and through the rain, I could see what looked like a million people crowded in front of a huge, slightly sinister-looking building. This was my first sight of Wigan Casino. It made me forget about the rain and the cold, it seemed to light up the dark night. I remember seeing the club's neon sign: the last two letters of 'Casino' were not working, so it read: 'Casi Club'. And that's how it stayed for the next six years.

In the rugby scrum at the main doors, we talked to strangers as though they were old friends. The expectation was infectious, it buzzed through the throng as lads from towns hundreds of miles apart hugged like long-lost brothers. Faces were animated with excitement and the conversation glowed with happiness. Girls laughed loudly at some tit-bit of news, and everywhere you looked, people smiled back at you. It was wonderful.

Until we got inside the doors, that is. On producing our tickets, we were told that they were forgeries. We found ourselves ejected back out onto the pavement as the multitude poured into the club. By now, it was almost 3am and we had no money, no tickets and no chance of getting in. For good measure, the rain started again, and soon it became a good old Lancastrian down-pour.

Needing somewhere to shelter, we ran up the alley-way at the side of the club and ducked into a doorway. From there, we could hear the music throbbing against the club's walls from within, making us feel even lower.

The best idea that we could come up with was to find someone we knew, which we eventually did. Sitting in a small corridor at the back of the main building which actually led to the club's smaller sister – Mr M's – were several others from Wolverhampton who had also fallen foul of a rip-off ticket merchant.

We sat there for a while, covering the panelled walls with graffiti, and moaning to ourselves. Paddy Jennings announced that he wished he had stayed at home in order to 'shag his fist'.

Suddenly, two girls came into the corridor and approached us excitedly. In an accent wider than the Grand Canyon, one of them said: "Are you alright chuck? Can you not get in, you?" We explained about the tickets.

"Oh aye! There's loads of folk in the same boat lads. Don't worry, we'll get you in!"

With that she asked for our black felt pen (the graffiti-maker) and took my arm. On my wrist she drew a series of lines and letters, then smudged them together. I thought it must have been some quaint northern custom, but Steve understood immediately.

Once outside, he stripped down to a t-shirt, so I followed suit. Then he scooped a handful of rain water out of a puddle and smeared it over his face. I copied him. Together with the two girls (from Burnley, as it turned out) we entered the club and showed our forged pass-out stamps to the doormen.

The same bouncer who had earlier thrown me out from the club, was standing at the foot of the large staircase which led to the main room. He had obviously seen so many faces that night that he showed no flicker of recognition.

"Straight up the stairs, please, no hanging about". We did not need telling twice. I paused only to plant a big sloppy kiss on the lips of my new-found friend from Burnley, before bolting up those famous stairs for the first time.

At the top of the stairs there was a small corridor which had the manager's office on the left, and a set of double doors at the end. When I think about the Casino these days, the thing that always comes into my mind is the memory of standing at the doors, about to enter the main room. To those who remember the experience, two things will always stay in the memory as you pushed through, the blast of heat as you entered, and the smell. It was a smell born of thousands of sweaty bodies that had graced the dance floor over the years, of cigarette smoke, of Brut deodorant and talcum powder that had been put on parts of the floor to stop dancing feet sticking to the old wood. Smells can remind you of places better than photographs, but I've never experienced that smell anywhere else.

Standing on the edge of the floor looking at the mass of gyrating bodies, it began to sink in, just what the scene was all about. These were the best dancers, the most fashionable dressers and the coolest guys and chicks to be found anywhere on the planet. And finally, I was part of it.

I can't remember who was DJ'ing at the time, but I do remember him playing Connie Clark's "My Sugar Baby", and that was the first record that I ever danced to on that wonderful floor. After that record, the big gold curtains were drawn back, and the live act came on.

Tommy Hunt was a small-time singer by contemporary standards, having had a few small hits in the US during the '60s, but he had been adopted by the Northern Soul scene. His act, what I can recall of it, was enthusiastic and soulful, just what was required. But what I remember more, was what followed, the 'Dancer of the Year' contest.

There were six finalists who had all won through by winning the heats, which had taken place at earlier all-nighters. These kids were brilliant; their spinning, footwork and acrobatics were perfect and I was spellbound. Eventually they were whittled down to three, and the lad who finally won embraced the other two with warmth and friendship.

The rest of the night passed quickly. I recall going into the smaller room for a while (Mr M's, the 'oldies' room) and, as the morning light streamed through the club, I remember standing on the balcony and watching all those people dancing, an incredible warmth and good feeling coming from the floor. The lasting impression from that first night was one of coming home, finding where I belonged and where I wanted to be. I think I knew even then, at just fourteen-years-old, that I would never give up the Northern Soul scene.

In my first year, I heard so many records which were new to me that it's hard to list them all. The songs played in the local discos, and which had first grabbed my interest, were not the up-to-date monsters being played at Wigan, so subsequently my favourites from 1975 were mostly records which had been played at earlier soul venues such as the Golden

*The sounds I grew up with. A few of the early dance floor monsters from the Casino's first two years,
as played by Russ Winstanley for the soul-hungry crowds who flocked to the club in their thousands.*

Torch in Stoke-on-Trent, the Twisted Wheel in Manchester and the Catacombs in my home town of Wolverhampton.

As far as the Casino DJs were concerned, the biggest records of 1975 included the Three Degrees' "Contact" (Warner Bros), J. J. Barnes' "Our Love Is In The Pocket" (Revilot), Clarence Jackson's "If It Don't Fit, Don't Force It" (Valtone), the Flirtations' "Stronger Than Her Love" (Festival), Jeanette Williams' "All Of A Sudden" (Back Beat) and the unusual "I'm Your Pimp" by Skullsnaps (GSF). This last one was a biggie for John Vincent, and it typified the type of sound that he played; not the normal 'love song' type of soul, but something unusual and a lot more challenging. If you've ever heard some of the other stuff that John discovered, you'll know what I mean! "Zola" by King Errison is a perfect example, a 100-mile-per-hour instrumental featuring frantic bongo drums; and the Eighth Avenue Band's "The Whole Thing", which was originally from a US television commercial for Alka-Seltza!

The other main room DJs were Russ Winstanley (co-founder of the Casino with Mike Walker and Gerry Marshall), Allan Rhodes and the best DJ ever to work at the 'Heart of Soul', Richard Searling. Wolverhampton's own Pep made guest appearances and the oldies spots were supplied by Keith Minshull and Dave Evison.

MY TOP TEN FOR 1975

1	Billy Woods	"Let Me Make You Happy"	(Sussex)
2	Detroit Executives	"Cool Off"	(Pameline)
3	Larry Santos	"You've Got Me Where You Want Me"	(Evolution)
4	Van Dykes	"Save My Love For A Rainy Day"	(Mala)
5	Bits 'n' Pieces	"Keep On Running Away"	(Nasco)
6	G. Davis & R. Tyler	"Hold On Help Is On The Way"	(Parlo)
7	Malibus	"Gee Baby (I Love You)"	(Sure-Shot)
8	Bobby Hutton	"Lend A Hand"	(ABC)
9	Mel Britt	"She'll Come Running Back"	(FIP)
10	Jades	"I'm Where It's At"	(Night Life)

Chapter Two SOUL SELF-SATISFACTION

AFTER THE FIRST visit to the Casino, I was completely hooked. I made three or four further visits in '75, but this time, Steve and I booked a seat on the coach which ran every Saturday night from Wolverhampton bus station.

This was organised by a local lad called Gethro, a very well-known face on the Wigan scene, and one of those who had danced on *Top Of The Pops* to "Footsie". That coach was my introduction to many of the colourful characters who, like me, lived and breathed Northern Soul.

I can still remember people like 'Mad Val' from Droitwich, Maggie Duffy, Mick Davis from Kidderminster, Boris who dressed from head to toe in black at every all-nighter, Simon from Dudley – a brilliant dancer – and the plethora of Wolvo lads: Patto, Paddy Jennings, Jacko, Rob Samuels and John Caddick. The list is endless.

By the turn of the year, I felt one of the crowd, a regular. Saturdays would be spent hanging around the various haunts favoured by our set: Sundown Records which had a basement selling the latest Northern Soul pressings; the Chelsea Coffee House where we would meet to discuss the coming night; and in the evening the Octopus, a tiny pub with a disco which was usually packed to the rafters with 'soulies' clutching their Adidas bags. Until 10.30pm, when the mass exodus to the bus station came!

It is interesting to mention here that the Wolvo coach was used by a couple of people who went on to achieve fame in later life. Steve Strange, who had chart success with Visage in the early '80s during the New Romantic era, used to join us at Knutsford service station and another '80s icon, (who was once a rabid soulie) called Marc Almond also travelled with us on occasion. I was sad to read an interview with Marc during his Soft Cell days, in which he ran the Northern scene down. He claimed that Northern Soul was not real music, and that he had only been a 'little boy' when he was into it. It might be thought ironic, then, that Soft Cells' biggest hits were both cover versions of Northern Soul records: "Tainted Love", first recorded by Gloria Jones in 1966, and Judy Street's "What", a massive Wigan record in 1977.

Wigan brought together such a diversity of people that it was inevitable that differences of musical opinion would occur. Some of these would grow into slanging matches between DJs and dancers, both of whom thought that their particular musical policy was what was best for the scene.

The main argument concerned the direction that Wigan should take regarding new records being introduced by the DJs. Historically, the Northern Soul scene played '60s American soul music, most of which had never been released in this country. This policy was pioneered through the early '70s at clubs like the Torch, the Catacombs, Va-Va's in Bolton and Up The Junction at Crewe. There was so many undiscovered sounds waiting to be played, that the same musical policy was used by the Casino DJs in late 1973.

However, some of the DJs began to move away from the '60s only mentality and started to play current soul releases at Northern venues. 1976 was a good example of this, and amongst the biggest sounds of that year were many contemporary releases. "You Sexy Sugar Plum" by Roger Collins, "Elusive" by Babe Ruth, "I Love Music" by the O'Jays and "Trouble Maker" by Roberta Kelly were all first played as US imports before their subsequent UK releases. Other records like Black Nasty's "Cut Your Motor Off" and East Coast Connection's "Summer In The Park", although not released over here, were '76 originals.

This divergence from the old ways began to form a two-tiered scene; the 'purists' who would only dance to '60s soul, and the new breed who preferred the more funk-orientated '70s sounds.

DJs Ian Levine and Colin Curtis were at the forefront of the '70s revolution. They instigated the change of musical policy at the now legendary Highland Room at Blackpool Tiffany's, known better as the Blackpool Mecca. At that time, Levine was just starting out on what was to become a very successful career as a record producer, and his early offerings (mostly penned with Danny Leake) were, ironically, massive hits at Wigan Casino. Records like Evelyn Thomas' "Doomsday" and "Weak Spot", L. J. Johnsons' "Your Magic Put A Spell On Me", Barbara Penningtons' "I Can't Erase The Thought Of You" and the Exciters' "Reaching For The Best" were all dance floor packers – tailor-made Northern Soul, you might say!

Amongst the '60s stalwarts was Soul Sam. This much respected DJ had been on the club scene since the early sixties and is still an important figure on today's scene. He and Levine became symbolic of the opposite ends of the spectrum of what was or was not Northern

Soul. As far as the '60s records were concerned, Sam gave a pretty good argument in favour of keeping Northern Soul firmly rooted in obscure, black '60s material. This was the year that songs like Gwen Owens "Just Say You're Wanted" first filled dance floors, not to mention classics like Ron Holden's "I'll Forgive And Forget", Bernie Williams' "Ever Again", Milton Wright's "I Belong To You", Al De Lory's "Right On", MVPs' "Turning My Heartbeat Up" and the brilliant Herbert Hunter's "I Was Born To Love You". Most of these tracks were first discovered by Sam and the other regular DJs at the famous Cleethorpes Pier all-nighter, a fact that sometimes gets overlooked by those who only remember hearing them at the Casino.

At Wigan itself, it was pretty much business as usual, regardless of what different sections of the dancefloor would or would not dance to. Sixties and seventies soul were played side by side; you could hear Otis Blackwell's "It's All Over Me" played after the Rimshots' recent 45 "Do What You Feel" and both would fill the floor. The controversy which was raging between the DJs over '60s and '70s soul largely went over the heads of the dancers. We were not really bothered about musical dogma, Wigan was still the 'Heart of Soul' and nothing was going to spoil it for us, especially with what seemed to most of us like a lot of fuss over nothing, fuelled, it might be said, by personal dislikes which had nothing to do with musical direction.

Another bone of contention at the Casino was the growing unease over the mix of old and new '60s records. To the uninitiated this may sound rather an odd statement, but basically, 'oldies' were records which had been played on the scene for some time, as opposed to 'newies', which were the records being broken by the top DJs as 'new', be they '60s or '70s. Of course, to someone who has never heard a particular record before, it is brand new whether it was recorded in 1976 or 1966!

The Casino already had its oldies scene in the smaller room, Mr M's, playing exclusively tracks first aired at the Wheel, Catacombs and the Torch. This room was extremely popular with regulars. It was first opened as an overspill on the first anniversary night, and had a great atmosphere when it was packed, which was virtually every week.

In February of 1976, Wigan held its first ever Oldies All-nighter, in which oldies would be played in both rooms. So as not to interfere with the regular Saturday all-nighter, it was held on the first Friday of that and every month thereafter. Needless to say, the idea went down rather well. The first night was packed, and subsequent nights were more like anniversaries, such was the volume of people attending. Perhaps its instant success was due to a lot of people returning to the scene; people who had previously been disillusioned at the change in musical policy by some DJs, and given up Northern Soul altogether. If, as I suspect, that is what Mike Walker had in mind when he started the oldies nights, it showed another excellent move on his part. To keep the Casino open, it had to be a financial success. The Oldies All-nighter would ensure that this was the case until the very last month at Wigan, five years later.

With so many different factions of musical preference amongst the Wigan regulars at that time, and with the introduction of the Oldies All-nighter, 1976 was a watershed in the Casino's history. Other venues around the country were doing good business: St. Ives Recreation Centre in Cambridgeshire was hailed as the new Casino by its fans; Cleethorpes all-nighters moved from the pier to the Winter Gardens and began to attract large crowds; and in Yate, near Bristol, all-nighters started under the banner of the Southern Soul Club. Meanwhile, Northern Soul had dropped out of the limelight in the national music press. Pye Records stopped the Disco Demand label, and the world was spared further releases by Wigan's Ovation as Spark Records also pulled the plug.

None of this was seen as bad news by the soul devotees who still filled the dancefloors each week. The Northern Soul scene, we argued, was always meant to be an underground scene – we were elitist and proud of it. The world had taken a brief look at our music and now we wanted it back.

The summer of '76, you may remember, was long and hot and during those summer months, all-nighters at Wigan were stifling. On packed nights during that heatwave, if you stood at the back of the balcony in the main room, you could see a pall of steam rising from the dancefloor and collecting just below the ceiling. It would become so thick that you literally could not see the ceiling after a few hours. This condensation would evaporate when it hit the cold ceiling, with the result that drops of water, coloured dirty brown from years of cigarette smoke would fall on to the dancers below. In the morning, you could see soulies emerging into the sunlight with big brown stains on their clothing.

The heatwave continued into September, the anniversary month. This year, I had decided not to risk another rip-off ticket fiasco, and I made sure that the one I had was genuine. In the nights leading up to the anniversary, there had been much talk of the Casino allowing television cameras to film an all-nighter for a documentary about Northern Soul and Wigan. This, again, caused much heated debate among regulars, some saying that it would be a good thing to show the world what really went on there, to kill off some of the ridiculous rumours that went around about us. (Someone actually asked me once if it was true that we lay around all night whilst drug pushers injected us with heroin!) Others, mainly die-hard '60s purists, said that it would do nothing but harm; the media could get stuffed, we didn't need them, in fact, we never had. In the event, the purists need not have worried. Early the following year, when the cameras finally came, the end result was the finest most accurate account of the real Wigan Casino.

The third anniversary was fantastically well attended, as everyone knew it would be, and thanks to my genuine ticket, I got into the Casino early. The customary scrum on the pavement outside was as boisterous as ever, this time though there were no problems getting up those famous stairs.

At this stage of my soul career, I was very much into the collecting side. For hundreds like me, the record bar, which was really the booze bar – though never used as such – was the first place to head for. In that room at the back of the main hall, I met the créme de la crème of all the collectors, DJs and fellow enthusiasts that it became my privilege to call friends, over my time at the Casino.

There were literally hundreds of sale boxes to look at, both small and large. It became one of the most enjoyable parts of the whole night to stand and browse through them, talking about one record or another to the sellers, or finding some long sought after gem. I can remember lots of times when I would go into the bar with £20 or £25, an absolute fortune in those days, and leave several hours later with an empty wallet, an armful of records and three or four new friends! After this it was straight onto the dance floor, the only problem being to find somewhere safe to put the recent acquisitions!

It was at the third anniversary that I first met Dave Evison. He was in the record bar talking to a collector, a pile of records under one arm and a holdall under the other. This remains my abiding memory of

'Evo'; always talking records or Stoke City FC – you had to forgive him the latter! We got chatting about a record I was buying, I think it was Nella Dodds' "Come Back Baby" on Wand, and he told me he remembered the first time it had been played at the Torch all-nighter. I could have listened to people like Dave, Brian Rae, Keith Minshull and the other jocks all night as they reminisced about the scene's early days. I was eager to know as much as possible about the roots of Northern Soul, it seemed important to understand where this music came from. That may sound a little pompous, coming from a lad three months short of his sixteenth birthday, but I had already decided that there would never be another music which would get to me as much as this, so I wanted to know everything.

One of the things I remember about that night was going into Mr M's, the oldies room. Ask any of the M's regulars what they recall about it and you will probably get a dozen different answers. The heat, the crowded, cramped dance floor, the steam rising above the dancers. But there are two things that come to my mind when I think of M's. One was the bloody, great hole in the floor at the back of the room, caused by an equally large hole in the roof above it, which allowed rain water to drip down and warp the wooden floor, and the other is the instrumentals. I doubt if it was the policy of the M's DJs, but there always seemed to be an instrumental playing when I went in there. Records like the Fabulous Blades' "Jerk, Baby Jerk", the Crusaders' "Put It Where You Want It" – a brilliant jazz-type sound, Bob & Earl's "My Little Girl", and who could ever forget the totally insane "Scratchy" by Travis Wammack?

One record I recall that night in M's was Gloria Jones' "Come Go With Me" (Uptown), because it was the first time I had ever heard it. Kenny Spence, who is sadly no longer with us, was the DJ, and as he introduced it as Gloria Jones, I was expecting her classic "Tainted Love", but as the intro played, I was totally mesmerized by this new (to me, anyway) sound. I remember rushing over to the decks as fast as the throng would allow, and asking Kenny if it was rare, where it had been played, who had first played it, where I could get hold of a copy, and…when he eventually calmed me down, he pointed me in the direction of the record bar and said: "Try in t'bar, lad. It's not that rare, you'll get one f' next to nowt!!" So it was that I spent the rest of that night asking everybody in the record bar if they had a copy for sale, sadly to no avail.

I learned later that the record had been pressed on Canterbury, and these copies were easy to get hold of, but I decided to wait until I found a copy on the original black Uptown label. I didn't think that anything else would do justice to the enjoyment that that record brought me. That was the magic of collecting. No other music could give me such a thrill, or cause so much frustration.

During a break in my frantic search for "Come Go With Me", I watched the final of the dance competition. The Wolverhampton crowd, were perched precariously on the tops of chairs and tables at the back of the room, as the contestants did battle. As in recent years, the six dancers danced to a couple of records, and then were thinned down to five, then four and so on. The last three were two lads and a girl, all superb in their actions and faultless in their footwork. The girl won the hearts of everyone in the building because of the huge smile she wore as she danced, but she was eventually consigned to third place.

That left the two lads to contest the final. Everybody there will remember those lads and what they managed to do in that final. It was quite simply brilliant. As one would spin, so the other would go into an acrobatic routine and vice-versa. The final was only supposed to last for one record, but it soon became apparent that these lads were not in the mood to concede first place to anyone. Another record was played to try to separate them and promptly followed by another. Finally, after much discussion between the DJs, the manager and the owner of the club, Russ announced that there would be one more record played and a decision would be reached for the sake of the dancers who by then must have been totally knackered! As he played it, he said that it was the only record to play considering the night, and the incredible atmosphere that these lads had given to the occasion with their wonderful dancing – Al DeLory's "Right On".

It came as no surprise to anyone that they still could not be separated. The biggest cheer of the night came as the combatants gave each other a sweaty hug at the end of the record, and Russ announced a dead heat: the £100 prize money would be split down the middle. It was a fitting finale to the best dance competition that ever took place at the Casino.

That was the third anniversary. The Casino was at the peak of its popularity despite the other venues around the country, and it seemed that it would go on forever. What we didn't know then was that, in the words of Bessie Banks – "The Best Is Yet To Come".

MY TOP TEN FOR 1976

1	Inspirations	"No One Can Take Your Place"	(Breakthrough)
	Herbert Hunter	"I Was Born To Love You"	(Spar)
	(I can't separate the above two records, any more than the judges could separate the two dancers in the competition!)		
2	Otis Blackwell	"It's All Over Me"	(Epic)
3	Al DeLory	"Right On"	(Capitol)
4	Milton Wright	"I Belong To You"	(Satirion)
5	Tony Middleton	"Paris Blues"	(Mala)
6	Lenny Welch	"A Hundred Pounds Of Pain"	(Mainstream)
7	Jay D. Martin	"By Yourself"	(Tower)
8	Gwen Owens	"Just Say You're Wanted And Needed"	(Velgo)
9	Bernie Williams	"Ever Again"	(Bell)
10	Ron Holden	"I'll Forgive And Forget"	(Challenge)

Chapter Three "BE YOUNG, BE FOOLISH, BE HAPPY"

1977 WAS THE year that I left school, much to the disgust of my English teacher. He was puzzled as to why I felt it necessary to forfeit the chance of staying on at school and taking and passing final exams. The reason, of course was purely financial, with a regular wage I could get to Wigan every week instead of once a fortnight. Also, my new-found wealth would increase my record collection.

That really was all there was to it. Wigan came first, second and last. So at Easter, I started work in a small factory alongside two of my elder brothers. The money was nothing to write home about, but it did get me to the Casino every week. And Saturday morning overtime meant a few extra additions to the collection, unless it had been an oldies nighter the night before.

This turn of events brought a showdown on the girlfriend front, however. I had been going out with the same girl for nearly two years, a world record for me and I think she had the idea that I would be saving for the 'bottom drawer', so to speak. When I explained that the only thing that I was saving for was a white demo of "I Was Born To Love You", she took exception for some reason.

I bet that there are a few ex-Wiganites out there who will be familiar with this conversation (which actually happened):

"I'm sick of you and your all-nighters! Every week you go out all night, doing God knows what!"

I counter this with the old standby: "Yes, but I always come home in the morning. Just like Lou Pride."

"Who the f— is Loopride??" By now she is getting rather belligerent, and the punchline is not far away.

"Well as far as I'm concerned, you can either give up Wigan, or give up going out with me." Then the dramatic finale: "It's up to you David."

Yes, the choice was mine, so I made it. "I'm going to miss you, Elaine."

Bye. The choice, as I saw it, was between living a normal life, settling down with a nice girl, saving for the future…or continuing the life that I had found via Wigan Casino. Did I really want to end up like half of my school year? The sad sacks who lost their virginity and got a girl pregnant in the same night? I still see a few of them today, married at

28

eighteen, two kids to feed by the time they were twenty-one, been nowhere, done sweet FA. Stuff you, Mr. Normal.

So back to Wigan it was. The rumours about the cameras being allowed to film a documentary at an all-nighter turned out to be true. It would be in the early months of the year, and the programme would be screened in the autumn. The purists moaned for a while, but not too loudly.

That night was unlike any other that I can remember at Wigan, perhaps because the cameras required the lights to be left on. It was a very surreal experience, rather like being under a microscope with the big black eye of the camera recording our every move. People just did what they always did – dance, buy records, talk records and dance a bit more. After a while, you got accustomed to the lights being on, which made it all more of a shock when they went out at about four in the morning, after the filming had finished. It just went totally black. Dancers collided, people fell over chairs, it was all very amusing.

I did get into the finished production though, even if only for about four seconds. In one of those incredible coincidences that life sometimes throws up, right after my appearance on the dance floor, the camera pans around, and there, sitting about ten feet from where I am dancing, is my ex-wife. Of course, we didn't know each other then, in fact we would not meet for another eight years.

On the musical front, things were hotting up. Wigan had been the number one venue in the country, and to most of us it always would be, but other nighters around the country were proving very popular and the DJs who worked them were playing some excellent stuff. Whereas in the past, the records played at Wigan tended to dictate what was 'big' nationally, the emergence of other venues such as Cleethorpes, Samantha's in Sheffield and the Yate all-nighter, along with their regular jocks, ushered in some competition for the Casino.

At Cleethorpes, Soul Sam was playing stuff like Bernie Williams' "Ever Again", Bobby Diamond's "Stop", and Billy Arnell's "Tough Girl". To counter this, the Wigan DJs, and Richard Searling in particular, began to dig deeper for unknown, unplayed '60s records.

I have heard it said (mostly by ex-Torch, Twisted Wheel or Catacombs devotees) that much of the new material that was introduced around 1977, were simply records that had been discarded by Torch, Wheel or Catacombs DJs as not being good enough to play on the scene at that time. I suppose this does hold some truth; I remember talking to Pep (ex-Cats and Casino DJ) then, asking about some record or other, and he said that he could have bought most of what was big in '77 five years earlier, but when he and the other jocks were playing stuff of the calibre of Jean Carter's "Like One", Buster & Eddie's "Can't Be Still", and the Checkerboard Squares' "Double Cooking" every week as unknown sounds, they could afford to pick and choose. By the same token, however, there were some records played for the first time on the scene in 1977 which would have been massively popular to any soul fraternity, at any time, because this was the year that rare soul got serious.

With the introduction of so many new and extremely rare records, this was also the year when the EMIdisc made a comeback. These were studio acetates, copied from an original record on to a steel alloy disc, and coated with a thin layer of wax. The finished product looked like a normal record, until you picked it up! I had bought one in 1975, an under the counter job from Sundown Records in Wolverhampton. My 'EMI' was Lou Pride's "I'm Coming Home In The Morning", which was my first ever crack-up record on the scene. And Elaine's swansong.

The DJs of 1977 obviously wanted to own copies of the biggest sounds of the day to enhance their personal credibility on the scene, so the EMIdisc flourished once more. Some DJs attracted derision over this. There was the story about the DJ who played, shall we say, a large proportion of EMIdiscs in his spot, and at Wigan one night a fellow DJ asked him why all of his records were on the same label, i.e. a large white sticker with biro titles!

The practice of playing unknown records under different identities was not a new one. 'Cover-ups' as they were known, had been commonplace at the Catacombs and at the Torch. The purpose of covering a record was two-fold. Firstly it protected the exclusivity of a record to a particular DJ. If a jock 'discovered' a good sound which became popular, it would be so much harder for other DJs to get hold of a copy if they didn't know the true identity of the artist/title/label, thus keeping the record unique to his spot.

Secondly, this secrecy would make it harder for bootleggers to obtain a copy to press the record for mass consumption. This happened time and again over the years. One week a DJ would have a monster hit on his hands, and the following Saturday the Casino would be flooded with cheap copies of his record, the result being that all the mystique over the record died instantly. The other result was that the original copy of the record lost its value. I have seen copies of big dance floor hits being offered for a fraction of their value only a few weeks after they had been pressed. The average collector didn't care that his copy was a £1.25 bootleg, he just wanted to own the record after months, and sometimes years, of dancing to it. Only the serious collector would fork out £50 for what could be bought for just over a pound.

The usual way to cover a record. First, listen closely to the vocals on your discovery, and think of another artist with similar vocal ability and phrasing. OK, now your masterpiece has its new alias. Next, listen to the chorus, which probably contains the record's original title, and try to pick out another line which is repeated alongside the title. Finally, cut a circle of paper large enough to hide the label and paste it on the record. Take care not to damage the real label, as this knocks the value of the record when you come to sell it later. Write the new identity of the record on the covering label in biro, not felt pen as the ink tends to sink through the paper and damage the true label. Then all you need is six months of hard work trying to 'break' the record to the dancers.

To the rest of the scene of course, the cover names of the biggest sounds were definitive. For some, the true identities of artists was confusing: Russ used to play a record which he had covered as Wilson Pickett called "The Shocker", and on the night that he decided to uncover it, and reveal its true title and artist, he introduced it as Peg Leg Moffatt – the real artist. Although the record was popular at the time, usually getting a good floor reaction, the floor just emptied. Later in the same spot, he played it again, this time though announcing it as Wilson Picket. The floor filled.

Later at the Casino, the identity of one record in particular was to become an obsession with dancers and collectors alike, and its final uncovering caused bad feeling, great surprise and the virtual end of the career of one DJ...but more of that later.

As 1977 wore on, the quality of the records played by the 'newies' DJs just got better and better. Russ, Richard, Allan Rhodes, Soul Sam and Pep were churning out gems like Lillie Bryant's "Meet Me Halfway" (Tayster), Pat Powdrill's "Do It" (Downey), Don Varner's "Tearstained Face" (Quinvy), Jay D. Martin's "By Yourself" (Tower), Jimmy Rae's "Philly Dog Around The World" (KKC), not to mention Cheryl Ann's "I Can't Let Him" (Patty) and Johnny Hampton's "Not

My Girl" (Dotty's). Richard Searling began to take the reins as number one DJ, not just at Wigan, but on the whole of the scene, as the coming months would prove.

One trend of the music of this year surprised many people, and that was the massive popularity of certain songs which, although very catchy and danceable, were not soul music. A very big sound on the dance floor during 1977 was Bobby Goldsboro's "Too Many People" (United Artists); certainly it was arranged and produced in '60s soul style, and yes, I danced to it like everyone else, but somehow Bobby Goldsboro didn't fit too well alongside Taj Mahal and Tony Middleton. (Call me a snob!)

Other pop songs like Lorraine Silver's "Lost Summer Love" (Pye) and Jackie Trent's "You Baby" (Pye) appealed more to the pop psyche of the dance floor than the soulful. All of which leads to another hornets' nest. Whereas past political arguments were born out of preferences for either '60s or modern soul, some sections of the Casino faithful were growing uneasy with the number of pop songs being dressed up as soul.

Most, if not all of these imposters fell into the category of the 'Stomper'. This type of record was usually very up-tempo with ample sax, guitar and drum breaks to accommodate the dancers. In a lot of cases, the production and arrangement was tailored to imitate '60s Motown or Atlantic, but there the similarity ended.

As soon as the vocals kicked in, they fell flat. You could copy a soul arrangement, but very few white singers could deliver a soulful voice. The exception being Rufus Lumley! His classic "I'm Standing" is a paragon of '60s soul. Who would have believed that Rufus was a white, fat, balding country & western singer?

This exclusive need by some, me included, for nothing but the original article – Black American soul music – may lead contemporary observers to think that the whole UK soul movement was inspired by some form of political correctness. Were we all really social workers, driven by collective racial guilt? Why had we turned our backs on the music of our own country, white pop music?

I think the answer lies with the individual. Wigan Casino had no class or race barriers. People from all walks of life attended, regardless of colour or social standing. The only thing that we all had in common was a love for the music. (Apart from day trippers, those who tried soul this week, punk rock next week and disco the week after. You know the type. Arseholes.)

In my case, and I'm sure this applied to lots more like me, I treated the music with respect because of its individuality, being into Northern Soul set me apart from the mainstream. I would treat my current favourites at Wigan in much the same way that another sixteen-year-old would rave about the latest release by the Sex Pistols or the Stranglers; with youthful enthusiasm, zealously extolling the superiority of my musical preference over all others. I don't think that I had any concept of what soul music really was until November 1977, when I saw the Four Tops live in Wolverhampton, but that story is worth a volume all to itself!

This awareness of the chasm which existed between the qualities of pop and soul music made some of us into rather vocal opponents of the pop stomper, and that year, we had a fair number of examples to moan about! My top five most disliked stompers were Derek & Ray's "Interplay" (RCA Victor), The Ellingtons' "(I'm Not) Destined To Become A Loser" (Castle), Paula Parfitt's "Love Is Wonderful" (Beacon), Muriel Day's "Nine Times Out Of Ten" (Page One) and Nightwatch's "Lips To Your Heart" (ABC).

I should also mention stuff like the Jewels' "We Got Togetherness" and anything played by the Newbeats, but despite these, the real music just kept on getting better: Danny Williams' "Whose Little Girl Are You" (Deram), Susan Coleman's "The Age Of The Wolf" (Remmix), Teen Turbans' "We Need To Be Loved" (Loma), Servicemen's "Sweet Magic" (Chartmaker), Shawn Robinson's "My Dear Heart" (Minit).

Another record first played that year made a massive impression on the dance floor, and unusually, stayed a top sound for the next two years. Paula Durante's "If He Were Mine" (GJM) typified the best sounds of 1977 – great mid-tempo beat, faultless vocals and overall atmospheric feel that was perfect for the echo effect produced by the main room's high, domed ceiling. Many people will tell you that this record more than any other takes them back to the 'Heart of Soul' and all those great memories.

And so the eagerly awaited TV documentary, *This England* came to the screen. The general feeling was that out of all that had been written and spoken of Wigan over the years, this was the closest to the truth, and certainly the way we ourselves wanted to be portrayed. I watched a grainy old video of the programme whilst researching this book, and seeing the footage of the crowds queuing outside, the dancers on the floor, and even the collectors in the back bar and the balcony view of the main room, it was hard to suppress a feeling of sadness that it has all gone. It must have been hard for people with no knowledge of Northern Soul to understand what it was that kept us going back week after week, year after year. That's why that particular documentary was such a welcome change to what had been reported about the scene in the media. Even if Joe Public didn't give a toss about us one way or the other, at least those who were curious could see that there was more to Northern Soul than the average musical fad. Not that it made any difference to the level of commitment and enthusiasm that had always been an intrinsic ingredient of the scene, we cared about the world's perception of us even less than we cared about Joe Public!

Whereas the documentary gave a realistic insight into the views of the Casino members, the others who featured in the programme, ex-miners and cotton mill workers among the town's older residents, were said to have given the town a 'kick in t' teeth' by portraying Wigan as nothing more than a 'cloth cap and whippet' society. Wigan's local press were up in arms over what they saw as an insult to the Borough's civic pride, and they layed the blame for the trouble squarely at the feet of the Casino and its members.

I might be tempted to wonder if the Casino's eventual demise at the hands of the Borough Council was in some way related to the ill-feeling towards the club that remained as a result of the Granada documentary. Luckily, I'm not cynical enough to suggest that such a responsible local body of elected representatives would be churlish enough to close down any establishment just out of spite. That is just too ridiculous to even contemplate. When the club was eventually closed, it was in order to give the town a very important new civic development. Wasn't it?

The Casino had more than its fair share of live acts over its lifetime: Martha & the Vandellas, R. Dean Taylor, Junior Walker, Edwin Starr, the Elgins, the Marvelettes, Major Lance, Jackie Wilson, the Detroit Emeralds, Archie Bell & the Drells, Gloria Jones and Betty Wright to name just a few. Betty Wright was, according to many, the best act ever to perform at the club. I did not see her Casino performance, as it came in April 1975, and my Casino years did not begin until September of that year. But I did see her perform at Wolverhampton's Civic Hall, a show which was in effect her dress rehearsal for the Wigan night, as it took place on the night before. Live shows were rather strange to me back then, I tended to feel that they got in the way of serious dancing time, but I can still remember parts of her show that were absolutely electric. She had an incredible energy and such a powerful voice that it was impossible not to get carried along by her stage presence. I can vividly recall her renditions of "Clean-Up Woman", "Shoorah Shoorah" and "Show Your Girl". "Danger, High Voltage" was an apt title for her album.

The highlight of her show was however, the song that became something of a Wigan Casino anthem in '75. I can only imagine what the Casino crowds' reaction was to "Where Is The Love", but it took the roof off the Civic Hall!

One very clear memory of that night was the look on the faces of other people in the crowd; remember, these were the people that I idolised and wanted to emulate – the soul crowd. I saw the faces of lads and girls who had much more experience than me on the scene, shining with more than just appreciation for a great artist: there was something there that looked like pure joy. It was as if they were on the same astral plane as Betty as she belted out the soul, as if they were all in the show together. Looking back, I think that seeing those faces, and feeling that energy, was the first time that I ever felt part of the scene, although its mysteries were only just starting to unfold.

It was in that same venue, that a very special night took place two years later; a night that would not only alter my perception of soul music, but change me as a person, and shape the person that I would become in later years…"Ladies and Gentlemen, THE LEGENDARY FOUR TOPS!!!"

Chapter Four "KEEP ON KEEPING ON"

THE DRIVE AND energy within the scene came from the grass roots support and enthusiasm of the dancers and collectors. Of course, the DJs and promoters played a major role in the growth and development of Northern Soul but it was the passion of the true devotees that kept it all rolling along.

One area where this was perfectly illustrated was in the multitude of fanzines that sprang up over the years. These were filled with record sales lists, venue reports, reviews of rare and obscure records and readers letters, in short, anything and everything to do with our scene.

The fanzines were made by ordinary punters who toiled over masses of typewritten pages, Letraset and photocopies of record labels. Not only did they have to be reporters and editors, but all the printing and distribution of the mags, usually through the all-nighter network, was also done 'in-house'.

The best one that I can recall was called *Soul Source*, put together by Nottingham collector Chris Fletcher. I enjoyed reading his editorials which came at the start of the mag. They were usually very straight to the point of whatever was the latest bone of contention amongst soul people, and I used this outlet to voice my opinions on a number of occasions via the letters page. The result of this grass roots involvement was that the people who attended the venues each week, be it Wigan, Yate or wherever, were the people who had the biggest say when it came to issues affecting the scene in general, and fanzines like *Soul Source* provided an invaluable chance for soul people to air opinions – not always complimentary – about the scene and the people who organised it.

Not that they needed much prompting to talk politics! There was always somebody, at every all-nighter, who felt it necessary to slag off either a DJ or a promoter for playing too many oldies or too many newies, or to moan about the state of the dance floor, or, in the case of the Yate all-nighter, to complain that the sun was shining through the windows at dawn, and ruining the atmosphere. I kid you not.

As far as Yate was concerned, things went from strength to strength. It had a good, regular attendance, a friendly atmosphere and excellent DJs in Ian Clark, nicknamed 'Brains' because of his blue spectacles, Dave Thorley, who was to be responsible five years later for Stafford's

Top Of The World All-nighter, the best venue of the '80s, Dave Greet, Tony Ellis, Mac, Hippo plus a different guest DJ every fortnight.

To Yate devotees, Ian Clark was the south's answer to Richard Searling, and it's not hard to see why when you consider the records that he introduced to the scene. Amongst Ian's credits are Larry Allen's "Can't We Talk It Over" (Green Dolphin), Lawrence & the Arabians' "I'll Try Harder" (HEM), the Appreciations' "I Can't Hide It" (Aware), George Hobson's "Let It Be Real" (Sound City), and two of my personal favourites, the Gambrells' "Jive Talk" (Pioneer) and the oh so soulful Ty Karim's "You Really Made It Good To Me" (Senator).

As 1977 drew to a successful conclusion, Wigan's regular Saturday all-nighters were as well attended as ever, and the monthly oldies nights were a roaring hit with the punters, both old and new.

5th November, 1977 was a very special night for me, and one which I will always remember with great affection. A gang of us, from Wolverhampton, had bought tickets to see the Four Tops in concert at the local Civic Hall, after which the last train would take us to Wigan. The four of us, Jacko, Dave Evans, Mark Morris and me, looked rather odd with our Adidas bags and leather trench coats compared to the rest of the audience in their evening dress, but our embarrassment soon passed.

The support act that night was a funk band called Rokotto, and they set the mood perfectly with a lively, well performed act. Some may recall that the band featured in one of the Soul Festival All-dayers at the Blackpool Mecca. And the rest of the show was absolute magic. Nobody who has the slightest affection for soul music needs telling about the Four Tops. They had stayed at the very top of the ladder through the Motown days of the '60s, and proved that they could survive without

Motown with a successful spell at ABC-Dunhill in the early '70s. The Tops were icons of the Northern Soul scene too, waiting for them to take the stage was like waiting for royalty to arrive.

Finally, to the strains of their 1977 hit "The Show Must Go On", the group bounced onto the stage. The four of us leapt into the air with

excitement, shouting and cheering for all we were worth, and drew concerned looks from the other members of the audience. What did we care? Let the stuffed shirts sit and play with themselves, this was something to shout about!

In my holdall I had a portable cassette recorder with which I used to tape DJs' rare records during their spots at the Casino. It was one of the old ones with a separate microphone, which was OK for taping at Wigan because I dangled the mike over the side of the balcony. Here in the Civic Hall however, sitting in a tight row of people, there was nowhere to set the thing up. So all the time that the Tops were on stage, I had the mike in my hand, pointing it at arms length to the huge bank of speakers. This of course added to the amusement of the other people around us!

The Tops went into "Baby I Need Your Loving" followed by the beautiful "Ain't No Woman". Looking at those guys performing songs which we had grown up with was very special to us. Their poise, timing and phrasing was immaculate, something which had obviously come from being together for so long. Even the stuffed shirts around us were beginning to loosen up a bit, they must have seen the quality before them even if they had no knowledge of soul music. They just looked so perfectly in control, the Four Gentlemen of Soul, taking care of business like they had always done. When the four went into a medley of their Motown stuff, the audience were all standing and dancing along. Less than fifteen minutes into their show, they had what was a rather conservative crowd eating out of their hands.

What followed next will stay with me for as long as I listen to music. After the huge round of applause for the medley, Levi Stubbs announced the next song as: "One of our very favourites." As the intro played, it turned out to be my personal Tops' favourite too. "Ask The Lonely" is a haunting, sorrowful ballad about the pain of losing a love. I had become hooked on it a long time before this night, and I'd wondered before we came if they would be singing it. When they did, it became the highspot of the entire night.

The harmonies of the other three – Lawrence, Duke and Abdul – wove a perfect pattern around the achingly emotional lead of Levi. It was as though these men were telling us a story. They were saying that this is what it feels like to lose your love, and every person in the room was listening.

I stood there, cassette microphone in my hand, mouth agape, looking like a half-wit. But I didn't care. That hypnotic voice just totally blew me away. I felt something for the first time, something that is now so hard to describe. It hit me on such a base level that it was pretty difficult to deal with – it needed more than my normal senses. I had no previous experience to draw on, I felt detached from myself, that's the only way that I can describe it. As the guys sang the last heart-wrenching chord of the song, I came back to planet Earth with tears streaming down my face, and I didn't give a shit who was watching.

Since that night I've played the tape many times and it still has the same effect on me. Once I timed the standing ovation that followed the song, it lasted almost two minutes.

The rest of the show went by in a blur; the hits were all there, "Reach Out", "I Can't Help Myself", "Bernadette", "I'll Turn To Stone". We all danced in the aisles and in front of the stage, even the most uptight of the stuffed shirts let their hair down. But nothing could equal that feeling I got from "Ask The Lonely". It was just one perfect moment, as though someone had slapped me in the face and said, "This, my son, is SOUL, and don't you ever forget it." I didn't, and I never will.

The trip to Wigan that night was dominated by the Tops concert. The four of us told anyone who would listen about how good it was. At about 4.30am, I was in Mr M's, when the DJ Stuart Brackenridge, played "Since You've Been Gone" – a Motown side by the Four Tops from 1965. I listened to it with what seemed like different ears, although I knew the song well, it sounded somehow more intense, more emotional, as though I was hearing it for the first time.

This subtle shift in my appreciation of the music might sound irrelevant twenty years later, but at the time it was like a coming of age as far as my love of Northern Soul was concerned. It was as though I had been given the tools to do the job properly. To the outsider, the whole concept of Northern Soul is as alien as it could possibly be, so it is hard to explain something which is so intrinsically a part of soul music without sounding aloof or patronising to those who have never experienced it. It comes from within yourself, from the part of you that makes you unique; you don't listen to soul with your ears, you absorb it through your spirit. Soul to me is the spirit of one person trying to communicate with the spirit of another; the only way to listen to it properly is with your own spirit, your own soul. When you realise this, there can never be another form of music for you. Nothing will ever replace it.

Looking back, it is easy to understand why our contempories, punks in particular, made fun of our scene, and why Northern Soul was inextricably linked in the media with drug abuse. If you can't understand it, run it down – it's human nature after all! On the subject of drugs on the scene, I will say just this – drug culture in the late '70s was a very small fraction of the size of the problem that exists today. Drugs were part of the punk rock scene too, and also the jazz-funk scene, the disco scene and every other scene in 1977. Drugs have always been an integral part of rock music – did Janis Joplin, Jimi Hendrix and Keith Moon die of old age? I have always thought it very unfair that soul was singled out for criticism in this area. Whatever your viewpoint, Northern Soul cannot be accused of being the huge success that it is simply because of the people who wanted to use it as an excuse to take drugs. If that was the case, then why is there no longer a punk scene, or a disco scene?

Having being on the Northern scene since 1975, I believe that the secret of its success has always been its people and its music. The two both attract and compliment each other, soul music is only loved by those who are capable of appreciating it. The average punk would not really be able to get his head around something as sublime as "I Was Born To Love You", likewise a soul fan would find it hard to grasp the social relevance of "Pretty Vacant".

As I began to realise that my chosen music was so different from any other, I immersed myself in it and Wigan Casino to the exclusion of almost everything else. I wanted as much of the scene as possible, as quickly as possible.

Even as early as 1977, rumours were circulating about the Casino closing down. The idea seemed impossible. Wigan had always been there, surely it always would be. The world without Wigan Casino? No chance! I think the people on the scene back then knew that Northern Soul and the Casino was the best time that they would ever experience. In my case it was. It was something that I will always look back on with pride, passion and a sense of achievement, also a feeling of sadness. Not just for the passing of time, but for the loss of a part of myself – the innocence and security of youth which are replaced by the experience and responsibility of adulthood.

I had learned more about myself in those years that I had been attending the Casino, than in all the time that I had spent at school. Being amongst those people each week, and finding friends from towns hundreds of miles from Wolverhampton, gave me a confidence in myself and a dedication to the music as never before.

What lay ahead in the next three years for me, and the rest of the club regulars however, not only made us happier as teenagers, it shaped the rest of our lives. The Casino moulded people, just as other social institutions influence those who regularly patronise them. The 1970's saw the emergence of football hooliganism in the UK, and those who delighted in administering a good kicking to any person wearing the wrong colour scarf, found many a kindred spirit on the terraces of Old Trafford, Stamford Bridge and Molineux. Likewise, people who enjoyed drinking themselves into a semi-comatose state each weekend were sure to find a similarly incapacitated 'best mate' down at their local Red Lion or Kings' Head.

The patrons of Wigan Casino were not as a general rule to be found in either of these categories, nor were we classifiable as just 'nightclub' or 'disco people'. The average nightclub in the '70s had changed its traditional image of a 'sit down and drink' venue associated with the cabaret circuit into a 'get up and boogie' joint, cashing in on the world-wide epidemic of disco.

The trend had established itself firmly in Europe and America from 1974, when George McRae recorded what is reckoned to be the first disco record, "Rock Your Baby". The world-wide success of that record hailed the onslaught of thousands of imitators, some of which still sound good twenty five years later, although most have rightly passed into oblivion. If you think that is an unfair comment, then you obviously never had to endure "I Wanna Dance 'Wit Choo" by Disco Tex & The Sex-O-Lettes.

National musical trends being what they are, (over-hyped commercial ventures by mega-rich record companies) everyone wanted to be in on the act and the nationally controlled entertainment companies like Mecca found their richest seam of gold during the heyday of disco. Each and every Tiffany's club throughout the land packed them in each week and the national charts were full of groovy sounds. But the people who attended those discos were not soul people. I would not expect George McRae to accept responsibility for some of the lounge-lizards who lurked in those darkened rooms. The word 'poser' came in to to describe the stereotypical disco male; shirt open to the waist revealing large medallion, bouffant hairstyle held in place with hair spray, white flares and platform shoes, one eye in the mirror above the bar and the other on whichever chick was about to discover that this was her lucky night.

A stroll around Wigan Casino in 1977 would have revealed none of the *Saturday Night Fever* wannabees that swarmed into the majority of clubs that year. Unlike the commercial slaves who frequented Tiffany's, the soul devotees of the Casino were bonded by a common love for the music, rather than the need to be seen in a certain place, as trends dictated.

People on the Northern Soul scene tended to make lasting friendships among their peers, unlike the average disco cat who just wanted to screw as many birds as possible in order to enhance his one-night-stand record. Soul people were, and still are, the friendliest of any scene, even total strangers would become good friends in the course of one all-nighter. Perhaps this is because we were not restricted by the posers' etiquette which states that the only serious consideration in getting to know someone, is whether or not that dress or suit is real Gucci. Or perhaps the absence of alcohol at the Casino allowed its patrons to actually recognise each other two weeks running.

The upshot of this non-conformance policy by fans of Northern Soul, was that followers of other musical trends, unable to grasp the attraction of our scene, looked down on us and we were called elitist, as if the very term carried some sort of insult. Personally, I have always considered myself to be elite in so far as my exclusive devotion to soul music is concerned. That does not make me a musical snob, it merely confirms the timeless excellence of my chosen scene.

Northern Soul has always been elitist by its very nature. It is an underground scene which thrives upon its disregard for commerciality. Paradoxically, whereas the scene's first commercial venture – through Disco Demand and Wigan's Chosen Few – did much to enhance its stature, subsequent attempts at national recognition did nothing but harm.

The bottom line is, the rest of the world can call us what it likes, or label us whatever it pleases, Northern Soul has survived and will always survive simply because it keeps re-inventing itself to the 'elite' of each generation. The simple formula of venue, DJ and soul fan has never been bettered or equalled by any other musical genre, and when you combine these elements with the exclusivity of the actual records played, you add the mystery and spice that has always given soul fans that feeling of superiority over other musical fads.

The two years between 1975 and 1977 were my introduction to Wigan Casino and Northern Soul. If you had asked me back then if I would be here twenty-one years later, writing a book about the music that I love, I would probably have laughed. But as I was to discover, there was so much more to learn, so much more to experience, and so many more all-nighters to relish.

I remember the words of DJ Brian Rae at one Casino all-nighter: "I've been around for twenty five years and I'm still learning!" So, like many other soul fans of my era, I began to listen to people who knew what they were talking about. I started to ask questions about this record, or that label. And I began to learn.

Part Two
THE GOLDEN YEARS

"The people who found the records would only sell them to the top DJs, those whose reputations would help to break them to the punters. If you broke a record to the Casino crowd, you broke it to the whole scene."

EX-CASINO, CATACOMBS AND CLEETHORPES DJ
IAN PEREIRA, AKA PEP

Chapter Five "THE SHAPE OF THINGS TO COME"

THE DJ LINE-UP was always the most important factor of the Casino's success. There is no doubt that Wigan made the careers of Russ and Richard, but the quality of the supporting cast is often overlooked.

The faces changed as the years rolled on. Richard joined in late 1973 and became the eventual replacement for Kev Roberts, and a year later, Frank (Ian Dewhurst), John Vincent, Steve Russell, Alan Rhodes, Keith Minshull, Dave Evison, Brian Rae and Martyn Ellis all became regulars.

Most of these new faces already had reputations from their work at the venues which preceded the Casino; Dave and Keith at the Torch, Keith at the Twisted Wheel, and Brian from just about everywhere since 1966!

Mr M's, of course, had its own staff: Alan Cain, Brian Rigby, Mike Rollo, and some bloke called Steve Whittle, who was not only a superb oldies jock, but also one of my best friends from Wigan Casino. Not to mention Best Man at my wedding!

The M's main man was Kenny Spence, who tragically died soon after the Casino's closure and is sadly missed not just by his many friends, but by everyone who ever danced in that most famous of all oldies rooms.

Back in the main room, another DJ, who guested at the first anniversary, was Wolverhampton's own Ian Pereira, better known as Pep. I had been a regular customer in Pep's record shop in the town since I began collecting rare soul, and he had a reputation of having some excellent items for sale. Pep also ran soul nights at the Civic and Wulfrun Halls in the town, and top DJs like Ian Levine, Colin Curtis, John Vincent and Soul Sam were regular attractions.

Pep recalls his first visit to the Casino with great affection: "The main reason for my first visit (in late '73) was to check out the opposition! At that time, I was still working at the Catacombs and we had heard all the stories about Wigan, so I decided to see for myself."

As things turned out, Pep nearly missed his spying mission. "I had done my regular spot at the Cats the previous evening and, my wife Helen and I, decided to go to the Blackpool Mecca with fellow Cats' DJ, Basil. When the Mecca finished at two o'clock in the morning, we drove the short distance to Wigan. But by the time we got there, around half past three, I was absolutely knackered!!"

Pep and Helen stayed in the car to sleep off the previous nights' work (and alcohol!) and only Basil went into the club.

Pep remembers: "I remember waking up at about 7.30am and deciding to catch the last half hour. By this time, people were leaving the club, and all the exit doors were open, so in I went."

And his first reaction to what he saw? "It totally blew my mind! The floor was still packed and the atmosphere was fantastic. I remember the first record that I heard was Joey Dee's "It's Got You", and the combination of the crowd, the heat and the brilliant intro to that record just made the hairs on my neck stand up! It was obvious that this place was something very special."

Back in '73 however, the DJs were realistic about the expected life span of any venue: "No DJ or promoter expected an all-nighter to last for long. You have to remember that even the Torch all-nighters only lasted for about six months. The same is true of Va-Va's and Crewe's Up The Junction.

"The Cats is another example. We were catering mainly to an evening crowd who would be going elsewhere at the end of the session, so we knew that we could not compete with a venue which had an all-night license. Blackpool also had to work within the limits of 8 'till 2am. If an all-nighter ran for a year, it was considered a success."

How did Wigan become such a phenomenal success, given the fact that so many other venues had disappeared without trace?

"I think that the time was right for somewhere to take off in a very big way; there was a growing underground market for soul even before the national media attention that came with "Footsee" and "Skiing In The Snow". It just happened that Wigan saw this opportunity first."

Pep made several guest appearances at the Casino over the first couple of years, and was finally invited to do a regular spot in early 1976. By this time the Catacombs had gone; an all-nighter held in April '74 marked the Wolverhampton club's closure, with one of the guest DJs being Russ Winstanley.

"Russ asked me to do a full time spot every week, but by then I was already working at Cleethorpes and I didn't want to give that up, so we worked it out so that Alan Rhodes and I did alternate Saturdays which left me free to carry on at Cleethorpes as it only ran fortnightly.

"I was surprised that they let me do both venues: you could say that I was working for the opposition as well! Seriously though, I had a good working relationship with the Casino staff. The stories about the DJ's being deadly enemies were rubbish: sure, there was rivalry, everyone wanted to put one over on the rest of the DJs by having the best sounds or the rarest cover-up, but that was ultimately good for the scene."

Pep recalled how the DJs traded certain records in order to increase the track's exposure to a wider audience: "The classic example was Stanley Mitchell's "Get It Baby", we had that at the Cats, a year before Wigan played it. In fact, it was just about played out when the Casino DJs took it up, but I had to get another copy to play because of its increased popularity at Wigan. I'd sold my original copy when the Cats regulars lost interest in it, and Richard helped me out."

This co-operation between the top DJs did a lot to improve the quality of the records being played each week, and also gave DJs like Pep the chance to see their discoveries played to the scene as a whole, rather than just the venues that they worked: "I traded a lot of stuff with Richard. I sold him some of our Cats originals and he sold me stuff that we didn't have, like the Volcanos' "The Laws Of Love". It was nice to see sounds that we played first, go big with the larger audience as well."

Some of those Catacombs discoveries may surprise soulies who heard them for the first time at Wigan: Shane Martin's "I Need You" (Epic), H. B. Barnum's "Heartbreaker" (Capitol), and Don Varner's "Tearstained Face" (Quinvy) were all Cats originals, as was one of the biggest early floor-packers at the Casino, Danny Monday's "Baby, Without You" (Modern). Despite this, Pep remembers, the DJs of the day who worked other venues, tended to look down on the Casino as a young upstart: "It's true to say that some jocks ridiculed it, the standard of music in the early days came in for some stick. They would say that Wigan only played sounds that had been broken elsewhere, like the Mecca or Va-Va's. Some of the more established DJs thought that they did not need it, they had made their reputations without it and they could survive without it. But I think even the sternest critic would have jumped at the chance to DJ at Wigan, had they been asked."

The more commercial nature of Wigan as opposed to its contemporaries was perhaps the first reason for the divisions which split the scene in the mid '70s. The Casino brought new ideas, new

47

possibilities and a lot more people into the equation, and once the Casino had established itself, there was no going back to the old ways. Pep: "In the early days, Wigan was behind the Mecca and the other big clubs musically. The only records they played that were exclusive were things like the Sherrys and Dana Valery. Once it got off the ground though, it became the anchor venue for the whole scene. It had the largest regular attendance, the top DJs and the best records. If you broke a sound at Wigan, you broke it to the whole scene."

During his spell at Wigan, Pep played some of the biggest records ever to grace the venue. As well as the Cats' exclusives from his early trades with Richard, he is also credited with discovering such gems as Ann Perry's "That's The Way He Is" (Theoda), Little Joe Roman's "When You're Lonesome" (Tuff), Bernie Williams' "Ever Again" (Bell), (this record is often attributed to Soul Sam, when in fact Sam first played the Gene Woodbury version) and towards the end of his Casino career in 1977, Pep was the first to play John Bowie's "You're Gonna Miss A Good Thing" (Merben), Dean Courtney's "Love You Just Can't Walk Away" (MGM), Betty Lloyd's "I'm Catching On" (BSC), and Don Gardner's ultra-rare "Cheatin' Kind" (Sedgrick).

Amongst the hits, Pep also recalls one famous miss: "We had this record at the Cats in 1974, but I only had a master copy (a studio acetate copied from an original) from a Soussan tape." Simon Soussan became notorious as a bootlegger, although he was responsible for many great discoveries. "One night at Wigan, I was in the record bar when Richard came over and asked me if I'd seen the original copy of the record which someone had for sale. I didn't even know what label it was on, I had never seen a real one. I asked him who had it, how much, where was the guy? I was very interested in getting hold of it, but the next thing I knew Richard came back with it. He played it to the Casino crowd and the rest is history." The record in question was undoubtedly the Wigan Casino anthem over the first three or four years – the Jades' "I'm Where It's At" (Nite-Life).

People like Simon Soussan were the engine room of the rare soul scene; they were the ones who actually found the records in order that the DJs could play them. This they did by going to the source of the records: cities such as Detroit, New York, Chicago or Philadelphia. Once there, they sought out their contacts, often a bewildering network of people, who would get them access to warehouses, record shops,

LEFT: *Steve Whittle shows part one of his 'Before and After' advert for Grecian 2000. (Oakengates All-nighter, Shropshire, May 1998)*
RIGHT: *The first and last Casino DJ: co-founder of the all-nighters in 1973 and last man at the microphone in December 1981, Russ Winstanley*

distributors or even second-hand shops which had stockpiles of sixties records, sometimes tens of thousands of titles. If they liked what they saw, it was not uncommon for them to ship an entire warehouse's stock back to England.

Once home, the task of sorting the wheat from the chaff began. The good stuff would find its way onto their latest list (mailed out to their customers, or seen in most all-nighters) and the very good stuff would be offered to one or several of the top DJs, depending on the number of copies they had.

Giving first choice of the best records to a top DJ had several advantages. Firstly, the DJ would make the record well-known to the people on the dance floor and collectors in the record bar. Ideally, it should have been completely unknown to everyone before they found it.

Secondly, this popularity would result in a great demand for the record, a ready-made market for something which could not be bought elsewhere. That demand would be enhanced by the DJ until the time came to press thousands of cheap copies from the original to satisfy the punters. The DJ was happy because he gained the prestige of being first to play the top sounds, and the entrepreneur pocketed a few grand to finance his next trip Stateside.

It was the people who found the records who were in the position to dictate the direction that the Northern Soul scene took. The music was, after all, the life-blood of the scene, and a healthy turnover of records had to be continued if people were not to lose interest. Therefore, choosing the right DJ to play the best discoveries was very important to the men behind the lists.

This was a double-edged sword; as well as supplying the building blocks for the future of the scene, they also had to have a good financial return on their initial outlay – the trip to the USA, the cost of buying and importing the records – just to remain in the game. Not surprisingly then, it was good business sense for the background men to hedge their bets on occasion.

"When John Anderson, at Soul Bowl, sold Little Joe Cook's "I'm Falling In Love With You Baby" to Soul Sam, he already had 1,000 copies pressed up" recalls Pep. "All John had to do was wait for it to go big, via Soul Sam's work, and he had the product ready to meet the demand."

When records like Little Joe Cook's came along, the risks of the DJ not being able to break it onto the scene were minimal. "I'm Falling In Love With You Baby" shared the same backing track as the Sherrys' classic "Put Your Arms Around Me", so it already had one foot in the door. The Sherrys' track was, coincidentally the first record ever played at Wigan Casino back in '73.

Understandably, there was great rivalry between the various DJs as to who got first pick of the latest discoveries from people like Simon Soussan, John Anderson and Neil Rushton. To be offered the cream of what was a very good crop of '60s unknowns in the late '70s, only three or four jocks were in serious contention, and Soul Sam aside, a regular spot at the 'Heart of Soul' was a pre-requisite.

Pep: "In the early '70s, the top dogs were undoubtedly Ian Levine and Colin Curtis at the Mecca. They had the pick of the best sounds being discovered at the time because of their reputations. As the musical policy changed at Blackpool, towards funkier, '70s orientated material, Soul Sam emerged as the next main man through his work at Cleethorpes and Samantha's, so he would be given first choice."

Pep recalls how Levine and Curtis went about the job of picking through the thousands of imports that they had to work with in those early Mecca days: "The story goes that they would go to Ian's house for the weekend and just lock themselves in one room with a record deck and about five thousand imports! They would play the first thirty seconds of each title, and make three separate piles from what they

LEFT: *Ex-Catacombs, Cleethorpes and Casino DJ, Pep (Ian Pereira) cues up another classic at the Jimmy Ruffin promotion in May '98.*
RIGHT: *Northern Soul's most dedicated ambassador Soul Sam (Martin Barnfather), about to spin the Cashmeres' "Show Stopper" at the Oakengates All-nighter in May 1998.*

heard: 'yes, 'no' or 'maybe'." You can only wonder what gems slipped through the net in the 'no' category, given that the standard of the other two was so high!"

Soul Sam was the last of the better known DJ's to get to the top of the hierarchy without the aid of a regular Casino spot. As the reputation of Wigan as the number one venue on the scene grew, the jocks who worked other venues found it harder to get hold of those elusive top sounds.

At Wigan, the DJs began to form their own pecking order in terms of crowd popularity; Russ and Richard had always been the main pairing with the other main room men (Minshull, Rhodes, Vincent) as the support act, but over a period of time Richard began to emerge as the biggest floor-filler with his diverse and interesting playlist. Thus, as top DJ of what was certainly the top venue, he became the number one jock of the entire Northern Soul scene in the UK, and naturally the prime target for the background men to break their discoveries.

Alongside his DJ career, Richard also worked for RCA Records in the promotional field, and he was the brains behind the label's excellent

1976 compilation "Jumping At The Go-Go". The album featured the very best of RCA's huge '60s soul catalogue: Lorraine Chandler's "I Can't Change", Dean Courtney's "I'll Always Need You", Roy Hamilton's "Crackin' Up Over You", alongside more obscure tracks like The Bobettes' "Happy Go Lucky Me", The Cavaliers' "Hold To My Baby" and the superb Judy Freeman and Blackrock's "Hold On", with Richard providing the detailed sleevenotes.

Also working for RCA at the time was Soul Bowl's John Anderson. He and Richard were friends through their rare soul associations, and this working relationship was to become a professional partnership in later days.

1978 at the Casino saw the regular Saturday attendances fall slightly. This may have been due to the phenomenal success of the Friday oldies all-nighter, or the fact that with Northern Soul out of the limelight as far as the national music media was concerned, only the grass roots of the soul fraternity (whose numbers had fallen anyway from the halcyon days of '74/'75) still had the need for a weekly all-nighter venue.

Other venues around the country were also part of the equation, most notably Yate near Bristol, which had built up a loyal following of its own, thanks to the quality of the music and the venue's intimate, friendly atmosphere; a quality that was becoming more and more a thing of the past at Wigan as the warring '60s and '70s factions continued to bicker.

Yate had run under various names (Stars & Stripes, The Elite) since 1977, and in that time it gained a reputation throughout the scene as a model of how an all-nighter should develop; starting with a small attendance, and earning the respect and loyalty of the crowd with its basic format of good sounds and imaginative DJs.

Dave Thorley for instance instigated the 'modern oldie'. This was a record from the '70s which was not generally considered to be Northern Soul, perhaps due to its commercial success in the UK, but was well respected in its own right. A perfect example was Harold Melvin & The Bluenotes' "The Love I Lost", certainly not a rare or exclusive sound, but one which struck a chord with the receptive and knowledgeable Yate faithful. Another such track was the wonderful Miracle Workers' instrumental "Overture", which evokes great personal memories of the Yate experience.

The modern oldie idea was taken up by Wigan's oldies DJs too, most notably Dave Evison who made monster dance floor hits with George

Benson's jazzy re-working of "On Broadway", and Don Covay's 1974 top ten hit "It's Better To Have (And Don't Need)".

1978 then, with various venues around the country doing good business as well as the Casino, seemed like another successful year for Northern Soul. The only cloud on the horizon, apart from the growing divisions in the '60s versus '70s debate, was the mounting speculation about the Casino closing down. To us at the time, Wigan Casino was the Northern Soul scene, and despite all of its faults, life without it was just too awful to contemplate.

Each week it seemed that there was a new angle to the problem, and it didn't take long for the grapevine to spread the latest news. There were stories that Wigan Borough Council were to make a compulsory purchase order for the re-development of the site, and others that the Police were going to get the Casino's all-night licence revoked. On reflection, you have to laugh at some of the stories, even on so serious a subject. Heard the one about the American millionaire who was going to dismantle the building brick by brick and re-build it back in the States? All the people who had worked so hard to bring a little piece of America to northern England, might have been slightly miffed to see it all shipped Stateside.

More seriously, the speculation had spread to the national soul media. I remember reading in *Blues and Soul* that the date for the Casino's demise had already been set for September 1980, and although this was still a full two years away, it seemed like a death knell coming as it did from so authoritative a source.

Blues and Soul was always a staunch supporter of Northern Soul in general, and Wigan Casino in particular. In its columns, over the '70s, it was responsible more than any other publication, for the advancement of the scene. In fact, it first coined the phrase 'Northern Soul' in the early '70s, when legendary soul writer Dave Godin used it to differentiate between the more funky soul favoured in the southern clubs and the purer sound which was then exploding north of Birmingham. It is unlikely that Dave had intended to christen the whole scene thus, but the label endured, and was a perfect peg for the national media to hang their attentions.

Many soul fans will remember the famous full-page ad for the Casino which was carried by each issue. I can vividly recall going into W. H. Smith on a Saturday morning and waiting my turn to read it behind a throng of soulies who had got there first!

Blues and Soul was also a well respected forum for Northern Soul, and its columns, Dave Godin's particularly, debated both contentious and light-hearted issues surrounding the scene with equal attention to fact. It seemed then that everyone had something to contribute to the scene, whether their opinions were complimentary or derogatory. It is to the magazine's eternal credit that it kept its editorial views constructively critical, and remained a loyal ally to the scene and its members.

The great debate over the Casino's closing date would rage on for many months to come. When the doors did close for the last time, they closed on a scene that was divided as never before against itself, and *Blues and Soul's* forecast of closure had been out by over a year.

Despite the endless speculation, there were other things to capture the imagination of the Casino regulars back in 1978. The quality of the records played by the main room DJs improved noticeably. Although Richard was still way out in front of the rest, the others were at least giving him a good supporting act. Alan Rhodes, in particular, was playing some interesting stuff, and in my opinion he had taken over the role vacated by John Vincent in the main room.

To illustrate this, consider three records which Alan played in his main room spots during 1978, firstly Ernest Fitzgerald's "Ace In The Hole" (ABR). This was a contemporary release, uptempo and typical of the funky dance soul of the time. Not an instant candidate for Casino success, but a superb record which, as it turned out, proved very popular indeed with the dancers. Next, Southside Johnny & The Asbury Dukes' "I Played The Fool" (Epic). Another 1978 release, but the comparisons to the Ernest Fitzgerald track end there! I remember Alan playing it one night with the introduction: "It's not very often that we play records at Wigan which are in the charts, but this record is brilliant." And it was. It didn't matter that the Asbury Dukes were once the backing band for Bruce Springstein, "I Played The Fool" was the perfect all-nighter record; from the thumping drum intro to the wailing vocals, the faultless production and perfect dance beat. Had this been an unknown sound rescued from a dusty New York cellar by Anderson or Soussan, who knows how big it could have been. (I'm not parting with my copy, anyway!)

Finally, a record which I've mentioned before, Paula Durante's "If He Were Mine" (GJM). This was one of Alan's favourite Wigan records ever, and he played it in most of his spots – the perfect Northern Soul record.

Just with those three examples you have the full range of music that made up an average all-nighter, and I for one think that Alan was underestimated in his contribution to Wigan Casino.

Richard's playlist in 1978 confirmed him as the top DJ, and underlined the importance of his contribution not only to the Casino, but to the whole scene. His spot was the talk of the record bar amongst the collectors, DJs and punters who gathered there. By the very nature of being collectors, their interest was focused on wanting to learn more about their passion, and Richard provided them with a wealth of new material to argue about!

The desire to know more about the top sounds of the day, such as the real artists behind the cover-ups, the labels, producers etc, was given a keener edge by their rarity. It was unlikely that the average collector would get a copy of one of Richard's big plays until it was pressed, by which time it would be considered an 'oldie' anyway, and no longer on his playlist. In some cases, a record would be exclusive to one DJ because it was a 'one-off', in other words, the DJ's was the only copy in existence of that particular sound. Of course, whether or not the record was a genuine one-off was hard to verify, and the serious collectors would use their knowledge to eventually piece together the true rarity or identity of the latest cover-ups.

However, there were a few genuine one-offs over the years. Pep had the only copy of Don Gardner's "Cheating Kind" (Sedgrick). When another copy did turn up, the record was already a monster Northern record thanks to the exposure given to Pep's first copy by Richard Searling. Even today there are not more than three copies of the original known to exist, and "Cheating Kind" is one of the elite group of records that could be called super-rare.

In all areas of collecting, an expert on the subject will extol the virtues of the most sought-after items. The collectors of rare soul records were no less enthusiastic about their subject, and equally as eager to unearth an obscure original. As in all markets which are governed by the laws of supply and demand, the balance between what the collectors wanted and what the dealers could offer dictated the prices of the records. As the records became harder to find, so the prices spiralled.

The really big records, of course, were never likely to become available as the top DJs would be sure to check that a record would not suddenly appear in large quantities just as they were trying to break it.

And anyway, the DJs' suppliers would only give copies to a few jocks, no matter how many copies they had, as Pep put it: "There was a tier system in the DJ hierarchy, Anderson or Soussan only gave the best material to the jocks who had the credentials to break them."

This holding back of surplus copies of potential top sounds sometimes gave a misleading impression of a record's true rarity. Sometimes a record which had great dance floor potential was found in large quantities by an importer, even though it was previously unknown. Instead of the usual five or six copies which typically turned up of an obscure track, he was faced with 200, 300, or even more – sometimes the unsold stock of a small label would turn up in warehouses in New York or Chicago, untouched and neglected since the sixties.

Rather than miss out on a dead cert, our hero would ship the entire stock back to England, keep them until demand had gathered and when the time came, offer large quantities of originals to his customers instead of the usual cheap and nasty pressings. He also saved on the cost of pressing the record himself. That is exactly what happened in the case of the Ringleaders' "Baby, What Has Happened To Our Love" (M-Pac).

Regardless of how many copies of a top sound an importer was sitting on, the worst thing that could happen for him, and the DJ breaking the record, was for someone to find a copy and press it. The record immediately became useless to the DJ, because it was no longer exclusive to him, and equally useless to the importer who lost out financially, to whoever beat him to re-issue the track.

It was very much a partnership between the importer and the DJ when it came to breaking new material; both benefited from the deal, but more importantly, we the punters and the scene in general were treated to some incredible soul music. Between them, John Anderson and Richard Searling kept the rare soul scene from being swallowed up by the massive influence of the oldies all-nighter at Wigan. It would have been easy for the DJ staff to fall back on oldies instead of trying to break new records; the scene in '78 was dominated by oldies, from the once-monthly Friday nighter to Mr M's every regular Saturday night, not to mention oldies slots in the main room. The quality of Richard's main room spot ensured that new material, every bit as good as the oldies, continued to circulate.

Amongst the mountain of fanzines, tapes and records that passes for research for this book, I came across a record sales list which was

Paul 'Harpo' Harpin and Helen Pereira openly discuss abuse of alcohol, nicotine and good dress-sense at Burntwood Soul Night (June '98)

MIDDLE LEFT: *Some poser out on the floor in the main room of Wigan Casino (1979)*
MIDDLE RIGHT: *Home time. The Redditch crowd emerge from an Oldies nighter in June '80. My only remaining picture of Gabby from Bangor, she is dead centre.*
ABOVE: *A coach load of soulies at Stroud All-dayer in 1978.*

compiled by Midlands DJ and promoter Neil Rushton in early 1977. I can vaguely remember getting it from an all-dayer at Birmingham Locarno, a venue which was promoted, along with its sister all-dayer at Manchester's Ritz, by the Heart of England Soul Club, of which Neil was the founder.

The list has various sections: pressings, new releases and '60s soul originals, the latter making up the majority of the list. Under the heading of "RARITIES", these imported items covered three and a half pages, and catered for all tastes in '60s rare soul: popular oldies, obscurities, and many titles which back in 1977 were complete unknowns, never having been played before on the scene. Reading through the list twenty-one years later is like opening a time capsule. Comparing the prices of the records then and now is amusing, but the fascinating thing is seeing some titles which went on to become huge Northern records, which were probably passed over by the majority of collectors back in '77.

The records that Neil expected to go big were accompanied by the occasional comment, and these provide interesting reading in themselves; on a few titles, he revealed which DJ had already bought a copy, giving the collectors a tantalising chance to buy a future monster! For example, these three titles from the list:

- Robert Knight "I'm Sticking With You" (Elf) £15.00
  (*The above record is DYNAMITE, sold to Soul Sam – one left*)
- Fifth Avenue Band "One Way Or The Other" (Reprise) £7.00
  (*Get this while you can – two big DJs bought this!*)
- Edwin Starr "Don't Tell Me I'm Crazy" (Soul) £10.00
  (*Every DJ bought one – mid-sixties brilliance!*)

As a matter of interest, of these examples only the Edwin Starr track gained dance floor interest. Of the others, the Fifth Avenue Band was played some years later at Stafford all-nighter, but Robert Knight sank without trace. No prizes for guessing which of the three found its way into my collection!

Lists like this were good sources of advice when it came to the unknown legions of records that you came across in the Casino record bar. On a few occasions I can remember buying stuff which I'd never heard before, but the artist, title, or label was familiar to me from a record list. For instance, I took Neil's advice, from his list, to buy these three:

- Eddie Holman "Stay Mine For Heaven's Sake" (Parkway) £5.00
  (Soul lovers should buy this vintage sound – should be getting £20.00!)
- Epic Splendour "A Little Rain Must Fall" (Hot Biscuit) £3.00
  (Get this while it's cheap – it must go big)
- Tony Talent "Gotta Tell Somebody" (Vando) £4.00
  (Brilliant – a magic Van McCoy dancer – similar to Tobi Legend)

Some years later at an all-nighter at the Unicorn Club in Leighton Buzzard, a fellow collector called Tony Warot picked a copy of the Tony Talent record out of a sales box and asked me if I knew it. He had never seen the record before, but his collector's intuition told him that it might be good. With Van McCoy credited as composer, producer and arranger on the label, any collector worth his salt would have looked twice. It gave me great pleasure to pass on my knowledge of the record, and urge him to buy it, which he did. At the next Unicorn, I asked him what he thought of my recommendation, at which he shook my hand and said: "Dave, it's brilliant mate! It made the hairs on the back of my f— neck stand up!!"

Tony was a regular at the Torch when I was just twelve-years-old, his collection and knowledge of soul are legendary on the scene, and he remains a respected figure on the Northern Soul scene today. Being able to occasionally introduce a personal favourite to someone with his knowledge has always been one of the best things about collecting rare soul.

Finally from the list, this bunch of titles are the unknowns that Neil had the highest hopes for, the ones that were touted to the top DJs for their playlists. Some didn't 'go big', some got moderate dance floor time and faded into obscurity. Two of them however, achieved the scene's equivalent of number one. Remember that this is just one example of the dozens of lists that were in circulation during the Wigan era. To a large extent, these lists were the main source of the 'new' '60s soul that Russ, Richard, Soul Sam and the other top DJs worked with. Again, the accompanying comments reflect what the list compilers Neil and Frank, thought of each record's chances of success.

- The Isonics "Sugar" (Kammy) £6.00
  (Fantastic – will go big!)
- Our Ladies Of Soul "Let's Groove Together" (Kelton) £15.00
  (Our favourite – absolutely brilliant female vocals)

- Esko Affair "Salt And Pepper" (Mercury) £4.00
  (Sold to Soul Sam!)
- American Youth Choir "Keep Your Fine Self" (Polydor) £10.00
  (The above record is a great dancer – get it while it's cheap!)
- Little Big Horns "It Was A Very Good Year" (Crazy) £20.00
  (Monster! – remember where you saw it first – watch it go!)
- Ree Flores "Look Into My Heart" (M & H) £12.00
  (The above was sold to Johnny Manship two months ago – sold two since to top DJs, two left)
- Posse "Evil" (Janus) £20.00
  (This sold to top DJ for great price – one left!)
- Jimmy McFarland "Lonely Lover" (RPR) £20.00
  (Our no. 1 tip – Holland-Dozier-Holland, strings, vibes all add up to a new monster!!)

"Evil" and "Lonely Lover" were two of the biggest sounds of 1978 at the Casino, and their popularity carried through, not only to the close of Wigan, but even to today – perfect all-nighter records, almost tailor-made Northern Soul.

As you can see, Northern Soul and the success of Wigan Casino were not totally inter-linked, a lot of people worked very hard to establish both the venue and the music, and although each relied upon the other to survive, only the continued hard work of those people would ensure that the Northern Soul scene did not evaporate in the same way as the punk scene.

The unsung heroes of both the Casino and the music were, responsible for 'Keeping The Faith'. Too much praise can never be given to the men behind the lists, the promoters and everyone else who helped to further the cause. Very few people ever made a full-time living out of Northern Soul. It was a common love of the music and a desire for it to continue that inspired the scene and its members to keep on keeping on, whether at Wigan, Cleethorpes, Yate or anywhere else.

But as I said at the start of this chapter, it was the DJs who held the balance of power. They drew the punters to the venues with their reputations and they were the front men for all the hard work of the unsung heroes. Within the elitist world of Northern Soul, some DJs became stars, a few became legends.

The entire history of the scene has never produced a more legendary, more controversial, more charismatic or more influential ambassador than the quietly spoken history teacher from North Wales who went under the name of Soul Sam...

MY TOP TEN FOR 1978

1	Stemmons Express	"Woman, Love Thief"	(Wand)
2	Yvonne Vernee	"Just Like You Did Me"	(Sonbert)
3	Carol & Gerri	"How Can I Ever Find A Way"	(MGM)
4	John Leach	"Put That Woman Down"	(Lawn)
5	Rita & The Tiaras	"Gone With The Wind Is My Love"	(Dore)
6	Little Johnny Hamilton	"Oh, How I Love You"	(Dore)
7	Frank Beverly	"Because Of My Heart"	(Fairmount)
8	Kenny Gamble	"The Joke's On You"	(Arctic)
9	Jimmy Burns	"I Really Love You"	(Erica)
10	Charlie Gracie	"He'll Never Love You Like I Do"	(Diamond)

Chapter Six "FROM THE TEACHER TO THE PREACHER"

SOUL SAM, REAL name Martin Barnfather, has been at the forefront of the Northern scene since the early seventies. It is unlikely that anyone connected to the scene, past or present, has not either raved over his discoveries, or cast him as hero or villain, in one of the countless debates, to have divided the scene over the years. Whatever the issue, be it musical policy between '60s and '70s soul or the wholesale invasions of the scene by jazz-funk fans and the so-called 'Mod Revivalists', Sam was not slow to throw his hat into the ring, and his strong opinions sometimes exacerbated a situation; what were mere bodies of opinion turned into armed camps.

There is no doubt that Sam had the knack of making the average soul fan consider wider aspects of the scene than just dancing or collecting. I have not personally agreed with some of his views over the years, but I have never once doubted his sincerity in those views. Soul Sam gave the Northern Soul scene a conscience.

Considering the influencial role that he played in the development of the scene, not to mention the attitudes of many people on the scene, Sam has always maintained an air of modesty about his DJ career; there is no complexity to his personality, only a quiet confidence in his own opinion. I am sure that Martin Barnfather the history teacher deals with life with the same alacrity as Soul Sam the DJ. Even so, when I interviewed him in my research for this book, I was very surprised by the frankness and honesty of some of his opinions.

Sam declared: "I don't like all-nighters, I never have done. I much prefer the evening format which Blackpool Mecca had." Quite a surprise considering that he worked at every major all-nighter venue through the '70s and '80s, and still tops the bill at many of todays! "In the seventies, my favourite venue was the Mecca; Ian Levine was a trendsetter who had absolute conviction in what he was playing. There were no commercial pressures on him to play anything but the records that he wanted to play."

Sam believes that the early seventies clubs were the natural progression of what had started as the original Mod scene of which he had been a part of back in 1964/65 – an underground movement which was dedicated to finding its own music and its own style, regardless of, and indeed in spite of, any commercial interest.

"I was glad when the Mod scene died in the late '60s. By then it had been invaded by groups like The Who, who exploited its reputation to the hilt to gain commercial success. That inevitably destroys any trend, and the Mecca was amongst the first clubs to return to the underground roots of the music. For me, the Mecca brought the magic back."

It was with Ian Levine that Sam had the first and most famous of his many political debates over musical policy. Levine, and fellow Mecca DJ Colin Curtis changed their output from '60s soul to funk-orientated contempory releases in 1974. The upheaval caused shock waves in the scene, and the arguments that followed caused many people to split into one of either two groups – sixties or seventies soul. Sam went into print to voice his opposition to Levine's new policy, and the two of them became symbolic opposites, each championing their own cause.

"Some of the things that Colin played were good. I appreciated them as soul records, but I didn't think they had a place on a rare soul scene. Ian's new records though were just ultra-commercial, they had nothing to do with soul, and were little better than disco."

The dislike of commercial exploitation comes across as an integral

part of Sam's character. And indeed his basic belief that the Northern Soul scene should stay an underground movement was, and still is, defined by his achievements as a DJ. Although change was inevitable, Soul Sam believed that the scene did not have to give up its identity in order to change with the times.

On the subject of Wigan Casino, Sam has mixed feelings: "My first contact with the Casino happened before it even opened as an all-nighter. Russ Winstanley called me and asked if I would join him on the DJ staff. I think, I would have been his first recruit had I accepted."

Many people thought that Sam should have been involved with Wigan earlier than 1980 when he joined the DJ roster, so why did he not take up the offer?

"At that time in 1973, I was working at the Top Rank in Hanley, Stoke-on-Trent and I was getting £50 per week. Russ only offered £25, so I turned him down! Of course, I had no way of knowing how big the Casino would become; in those days, if a venue lasted for three months as an all-nighter, it was a big success." To further Sam's frustration, a few weeks into the Casino's life, the Top Rank was converted into a bingo hall!

There was no time to dwell on what might have been however. Despite his preference for evening venues, Sam found himself very much in demand with many promoters who were running all-nighters in 74/75. "In the mid-seventies when Wigan was taking off, I was doing regular spots at various all-nighters: the Palais at Nottingham, the Fleet Centre in Peterborough, Samantha's in Sheffield, St. Ives Recreation Centre in Cambridgeshire and, of course, Cleethorpes."

For me, it was at Cleethorpes that Sam reached the apex of his career, and the warmth with which he recalls those windy nights on the pier suggest that this was his spiritual home.

"Cleethorpes was definitely the best all-nighter that I worked at. The atmosphere was so relaxed and friendly, there were no arguments amongst the DJs like there were at Wigan. Because of this there was no hierarchy in the DJ staff, we all worked as a team."

When Sam did work at Wigan, the scene was going through big changes and this was also at the height of the 'Mod Revival'. With so many different factions all converging on one venue, the atmosphere at the club in 1980 was anything but harmonious. "I never felt that I was part of the Casino set-up like I did at Cleethorpes, there was too much controversy. I felt that I was always left on the sidelines."

With his involvement in the top venues, few would have argued that Sam was not the scene's top DJ at that time, and as such, he was considered first choice for the top new material. "John Anderson tended to give exclusive access of his best discoveries to whoever could best promote them. At one time I was considered to be top dog, so I had a lot of dealings with him."

However, being thus chosen did not mean that Sam would play anything that was offered him. One incident perfectly illustrates this, and shows how his idealism, like that of Ian Levine in the early Mecca

SOUL SAM'S FAVOURITE '60s SOUL DISCOVERIES INCLUDE:

Moses Smith	"The Girl Across The Street"	(Dionn)
The Twans	"I Can't See Him Again"	(Dade)
Gwen Owens	"Just Say You're Wanted"	(Velgo)
Little Joe Cook	"I'm Falling In Love With You Baby"	(Hot)
William Powell	"Heartache Souvenirs"	(Powerhouse)
Herbert Hunter	"I Was Born To Love You"	(Spar)
The Sequins	"Try My Love"	(Detroit Sound)
The Inticers	"Since You Left"	(Baby Luv)
Bobby Diamond	"Stop!"	(Columbia)
The Burning Bush	"Keeps On Burning"	(Mercury)
Little Tommy	"Baby Can't You See"	(Sound Of Soul)
Little Johnny Hamilton	"Oh, How I Love You"	(Dore)
The Cashmeres	"Showstopper"	(Hem)
The Dogs	"Soul Step"	(Treasure)
Damon Fox	"Packin' Up"	(Fairmount)

days, was more of an influence on his playlist than a desire to be top DJ. "John gave me the first copy of 7th Wonder "Captain Of My Ship", which he thought would be very big. When I played it through, I thought it was garbage. There was no way that I was going to play it, so I swapped it with Alan Rhodes. I have never put anything on a record deck that I didn't believe in, and I never will."

Predictably, 7th Wonder did go very big indeed, and was one of the first records to bridge the gap between '60s and '70s soul on the scene. These so-called 'crossover' sounds appealed to dancers on both sides of the divide; the purists recognised the heavy influence of uptempo Motown-style in the beat, and those with a preference for the funkier, modern approach were just as happy to get their Hawaiian shirts sweaty.

Another of Sam's dislikes was the oldies scene, which he felt did little to help the progress of Northern Soul. Although he himself was at one time playing oldies, he felt it was more likely to drive dancers and collectors away than attract new blood: "The success of Wigan's Oldies all-nighter led to a massive increase of oldies being played at other venues. This made the whole scene go stale. DJs began to choose the soft option of playing crowd-pleasing oldies, rather than trying to discover and break new records."

Wigan was also, in Sam's view, departing from the traditional underground image of Northern Soul, and thus hampering its progress, by its efforts to make the scene more commercial.

"The Casino management thought that the way ahead for the scene was to bring it to the attention of the nation. This may have been financially successful, and indeed might have brought new blood onto the scene, but in my opinion it was bad for Northern Soul. What happened was the people being attracted to the scene through its media coverage began to turn it into a dance scene, not a soul scene; despite their chart successes, most of the Disco Demand and the Casino Classics releases were pop records, and had little to do with soul music."

Casino Classics began life on February 3rd 1979, with the release of a three-track maxi single entitled "Three Before Eight". The title refered to the last three records played at the end of every all-nighter at the Casino. Eight o'clock was of course chucking-out time.

The three were: Jimmy Radcliffe's "Long After Tonight Is All Over", Tobi Legend's "Time Will Pass You By" and Dean Parrish's "I'm On My Way" all of which the average soul fan could recite backwards. None of them were rare records, all had at some time or other been pressed or re-issued, yet the maxi single sold over 50,000 copies in the UK. This success, similar to that gained in 1975 with the Disco Demand series, persuaded RK Records to issue further releases of material that was 'big up north', including Lorraine Silver's "Lost Summer Love", the Flirtations' "Little Darling (I Need You)" – a version of Marvin Gaye's Motown classic, James & Bobby Purify's "Shake A Tail Feather", and most notably a couple of monster dance floor hits, Reperata & The Delrons' "Panic" and the fabulous Geri Granger's "I Go To Pieces".

None of the above could be accused of being a pop record except Lorraine Silver's and all were very popular at the Casino at one time or another. However, the pop records that Sam refered to on the label did cause a few differences of opinion to arise. Some of these were specially recorded for release on the label by unknown session musicians and backing singers, which raised an eyebrow or two amongst the purists in the record bar. One of the early releases was a cover version of the Twisted Wheel classic "I'll Do Anything (He Wants Me To Do)" by Doris Troy. Russ had been playing it in his spot under the alias of Lenny Gamble prior to its release, after which it was discovered, to the horror of everyone who bought a copy, that the true artist was in fact none other than Tony Blackburn.

With material like that, of little or no interest to a seasoned soul fan, being promoted nationally as Northern Soul, perhaps the misgivings of

LEFT: *Harpo explains his choice of footwear. Casino main room, May '81.*
RIGHT: *Respect due: Keith 'Wagsy' Henry turns on the charm at Birmingham Locarno '82.*

some over commercialisation, can be understood; people who were previously ignorant of the scene and its music would certainly have been misled somewhat if they took "The Theme From Joe 90" by the Ron Grainer Orchestra to be the genuine article. Lovers of soul music are notoriously protective of their music and the artists who make it. This perhaps goes back to the early sixties when Black American artists saw their work stolen by white bands.

Whatever the connoisseurs on the scene – myself included – thought of the Casino Classics issue, there is no doubt that it was good business sense on the part of the management of the Casino. At the time of the label's first release, the weekly attendance of the Saturday all-nighter was still in decline, although the Oldies nighter continued to pack them in once a month. I wish that I could be more enthusiastic about Casino Classics, but being a dyed-in-the-wool purist, I have to admit that some of the labels' output did not do us any favours. In my opinion, the best thing to come out of the venture was that it persuaded Gerry Marshall, the clubs' owner, to carry on at a time when, with attendances down and rumours of closure rife, he could just as easily have said "Enough is enough", and opted for a quiet life.

Congratulations to

WIGAN CASINO

THE WORLD'S NUMBER ONE SOUL VENUE
ON YOUR SEVENTH ANNIVERSARY

FROM THE WORLD'S NUMBER ONE
SOUL MAGAZINE

BLUES and SOUL

A quiet life, though was not on the menu for Casino regulars in 1979. As well as the launch and subsequent controversy over Casino Classics, there was another invasion of the club later in the year by large numbers of youths wearing '60s style suits, parkas and pork-pie hats. This was the 'Mod' revival.

The fad began with the release of *Quadrophenia*, which was based on the original Mods of the early sixties, and told the story of the seaside battles between Mods and Rockers which had then shocked the nation. The film had the same effect as previous music-based works like *Saturday Night Fever* and *Thank God It's Friday*, it started a copycat movement of youngsters who wanted to ape the stars of the film. How many discos in Britain were packed with John Travolta wannabees in 1977? Unfortunately for us, the Northern Soul scene provided a ready-made time warp for those wishing to re-live the lifestyle of their mums and dads fifteen years earlier, and predictably, they turned up in droves.

Sam: "The whole thing was a hype. It was not a musical trend, just a result of media publicity given to a film made by a group, The Who, desperate to relive their past glories. The very term 'Mod Revival' is a contradiction: Mod is short for modern, or forward-looking, so how can they have been true Mods by trying to revive the past?"

Added to this, the sixties clothes served only to increase their odd image, though they did give the non-Mods a few giggles. One night I saw a couple of lads in full regalia carrying crash-helmets emblazoned with the Lambretta logo. All very smart until you realised that these lads were getting off a coach and neither of them owned scooters.

Unfortunately, their presence at Wigan caused a lot of bad feeling amongst soul fans, most of whom were sick to the back teeth of groups of outsiders trying to dictate the future of the scene to them. Worse was to come, as Sam remembers: "When the Mods came to Northern venues, they requested records from the original Mod era, which were not even considered oldies on the Northern circuit; records like The Kingsmen "Louie, Louie" and Booker T. & the M.G.s "Green Onions" were popular with them, but only because they heard them on the film."

Inevitably, another sell-out occured. "To their eternal shame, some DJs caved in and played that sort of thing at all-nighter venues, even Wigan's main room on the regular Saturday night."

Throughout this work, I have tried to give both sides of story as far as any controversial issues are concerned. My view is that whatever a DJ or promoter did to bring controversy upon himself, he did it because he thought that it was best for the scene, and as such he deserves respect for having the courage of his convictions. Accordingly, I accept that Casino Classics and some of the other media intrusions into our scene were, although regrettable, necessary. But I will never forgive Russ for playing reggae and ska during a regular Saturday all-nighter, just to appease a bunch of time-warped posers in fancy dress.

The night that the unthinkable crime occured was at the height of the film's media hype, and TV and radio were awash with fifteen-year-old film clips and interviews, about the Bank Holiday mayhem caused by 1964's Mods. The Casino was reasonably full and Russ was about half way through his two and a half hour spot which traditionally opened each all-nighter.

In the record bar with Paul 'Harpo' Harpin, I was browsing through a few sale boxes. I think we had been taking the piss out of Mods in general, and a few of the Wolverhampton crowd who had 'turned Mod'. Then it came: the screech of tyres, the Tommy-gun sound effect and the immortal line, "Al Capone's guns don't argue!!!". Russ was playing Prince Buster. At Wigan Casino. On newies night.

A roar of approval went up from the Mods, who quickly descended on the dance floor like a swarm of locust. Our dance floor.

Equally audible was the gasp of horror from the faithful. I have only ever seen a Casino crowd turn nasty on two occasions, and this was one of them. Harpo said "What the f— has he done now?", and there were a lot of other comments shouted towards the stage: "Get it off!! Turn the f—— thing off!!!" and, "What the f— are you playing at, Russ?" stick in my mind to this day.

I swear the volume level of the record dipped for a few seconds, as if Russ was trying to listen to the abuse of the soul regulars. For a moment, I thought he was going to take the record off half-way through, but he didn't. On reflection, he would probably have got even more stick if he had cut it short. It is hard to imagine that so small a thing as playing a record, just one record out of hundreds that are played in the average all-nighter, could cause such trouble. But it did. To us, it was like finding a McDonalds at the top of Mount Everest, it cheapened the experience of getting there.

"That's it then." said Harpo. "Next week I'm having a f—— pin through my nose and going punk." In the event, the Mods' influence at the club had been negligible, and they disappeared when *Quadrophenia* dropped from the media's attention.

Soul Sam's outlook on the scene changed dramatically in 1979; like Levine and Curtis in 1974, he turned his back on '60s soul in favour of contempory releases, a move which had those who remembered his views on what was known as 'the split with the Mecca' up in arms. The reasons for Sam's about-face were many and varied, but the Mod revival and the top DJs' reaction to it must have come high on the list. To most Northern Soul DJs, the Mods were just another facet of the scene that had to be catered for, even if this meant playing totally inappropriate records at all-nighters, but to someone with Sam's integrity, they were the scene's death-knell.

Sam's guiding principals were that the scene should not lose its identity in order to change with the times or bow to commercialisation. Having been a Mod in the early days, his progression to modern soul was not so hard to understand. The people who slagged him off for changing his musical direction entirely missed the point. Far from changing his views, he was being loyal to them. Sam saw the scene in 1979 as the antithesis of the true meaning of Northern Soul, so being an old-style Mod interested only in going forwards, he shifted his attention to the next stage, which was '70s soul.

A perfect illustration of Sam's frustration with the scene in '79 came at the Club Lafayette in Wolverhampton, at one of the regular Monday evening soul nights which were organised by Pep. Sam was the main guest that night, with support from Pep himself and several local lads. I remember seeing a large proportion of the Midlands soul fraternity, turning up in Mod gear that evening, giving rise to much hilarity and piss-taking on my part.

Sam's spot contained 100 per cent pure '60s soul, including just about every top sound of the day: Rita & the Tiaras' "Gone With The Wind Is My Love" (Dore), Little Johnny Hamilton's "Oh, How I Love You" (Dore), the Agents' "Trouble" (Liberty Bell), the Cautions "No Other Way" (Shrine), and two of the best '60s dancers for ages, which

Sam had covered up as Bobby Jason "All These Things" and Don Parker "Packin' Up Baby". He played these gems to me, Harpo and half a dozen others who bothered to dance. Wolverhampton always was a major centre for the people of the scene; our venues and our commitment to Northern Soul have always been a source of great pride. But that night I was just embarrassed by my own mates.

I was talking to Sam at the decks as he wound up his spot. He was followed by a local lad called Ian Tyrer, who, like Sam, had been a '60s Mod. His first record was Booker T.'s "Green Onions", which filled the floor for the first time in the evening. And it stayed full for the rest of the night. Sam loudly shouted his disgust: "Oh for Christ's sake!!! The bloody idiots!!!" Is it such a wonder then, that he felt it time to try a fresh angle?

As you may have gathered already, I was always a staunch '60s only fan. I was brought up on a strict diet of old Catacombs records and Tamla Motown in my pre-all-nighter days: that is what was played in all the discos and youth clubs in the town. So when Sam did cross over to modern soul, I was horrified. Soul Sam's name in a DJ line up always used to ensure that a venue would be well attended by rare soul lovers, and that they would be rewarded by the top '60s sounds of the day. The first reaction of people like me, who had followed Sam around the country, was how could he sell out like that?

"In 1979, around the time of the Mod controversy, I heard a tape of the latest records that John Anderson had to offer, stuff that Richard was playing regularly at the Casino. Amongst these were some modern soul tracks, including Larry Houston "Let's Spend Some Time Together" (HFMP) and Z. Z. & Co. "Gettin' Ready For The Get Down" (Columbus). They were so good and so refreshing compared to the rest of the stuff being played at that time, that I had to get involved with them. I thought that the best way, perhaps the only way for the scene to progress was with material like this."

With characteristic abandon, Sam announced his belief that '60s soul was dead and gone in 1979; there were no longer any '60s records left to be discovered in America that were worth playing. Logically therefore, the way forward was modern soul. This galvanised the '70s crew at Wigan, both on and off the dance floor, into more vocal opposition. There was one '70s only DJ in particular, whom I will not give the satisfaction of naming, whose only contribution to the '60s and

RICHARD SEARLING'S PLAYLIST IN MARCH 1979 WAS AS FOLLOWS:

Eddie Holman	"Where I'm Not Wanted"	(master tape)
Vickie Baines	"Country Girl" *(c/u Christine Cooper)*	(Parkway)
Little Ann	"When He's Not Around" *(c/u Rose Valentine)*	(master tape)
The Sweet	"Broken Heart Attack" *(c/u Chester Pipkin)*	(Smash)
Judy Hughes	"Fine, Fine, Fine" *(c/u Judy Street – "He's So Fine")*	(master tape)
Eddie Daye & The Four Bars	"Guess Who Loves You" *(c/u Frank Wilson)*	(Shrine)
Moses Dillard	"I'll Pay The Price" *(c/u Eddie Jefferson – "I Won't Think Twice")*	(Mack IV)
The Lovers	"Without A Doubt" *(c/u The Ballads)*	(Frantic)
John And The Weirdest	"Can't Get Over These Memories"/ "No Time" *(c/u Spyder Turner)*	(TIE)
Friendly People	"Nothin' But The Blues" *(c/u Lee Valentine)*	(VMP)
Al Williams	"I Am Nothing" *(c/u The Masqueraders)*	(Palmer)
Gary Sole	"Holding On" *(c/u The Agents)*	(Knight)
The Nomads	"Somethin's Bad"	(Mo Groov)
George Kirby	"What Can I Do?"	(Chess)
Frank Dell	"He Broke Your Game Wide Open"	(Valise)
Lester Tipton	"This Won't Change"	(La Beat)
J. C. Messina	"Time Won't Let Me" *(c/u Bob Segar System)*	(Tom King)
Billy Hambric	"I Was Wrong"/"I Found True Love" *(c/u Steve Mancha – "She Said Goodbye")*	(Drum)
Court Davis	"Try And Think What You're Doing" *(c/u Herbie Williams – "The Lover Who Loves You Not")*	(West Coast)
Joe Matthews	"I Don't Like To Lose" *	

More about this record, and the identity of the artist, later.

'70s debate was to stand in the aisle near the stage at Wigan and shout "Shit!" or "Total crap!" after every '60s record that Richard played. Such was the atmosphere at Wigan Casino in 1979, it was not just a case of 'us and them', but 'us, them and the Mods.'

Dave Godin of *Blues and Soul* once said that Northern Soul would always go through changes, but those changes would make it stronger. Ultimately, there would always be a soul scene because people would always want something better than the crap put before them by record company executives. To me, and thousands of my generation, Wigan Casino was the ultimate experience. Being a Casino regular was tangible proof of our individuality, and we preached the

Another ally to Wigan Casino, was the weekly Black Echoes, *which carried up-to-the-minute venue information, as well as excellent and thought provoking articles by well-known scene figures such as Pat Brady and Russ Winstanley.*

gospel of Northern Soul to anyone who would listen. For all its faults, Wigan Casino was the Northern Soul scene, or at least its biggest part, so even the uninformed reader can guess how it felt for us to see so many intruders fighting over what belonged to us. If this was the price to pay to change with the times, then to hell with change.

Sam, meanwhile, was severing his links with '60s soul, even to the extent of getting rid of his own best rare soul items; "I swapped my two biggest '60s cover-ups, which were Bobby Jason and Don Parker, with Richard for Z. Z. & Co. and Larry Houston. After that, I was only interested in finding new '70s material, and I rate stuff like Prince Phillip Mitchell "I'm So Happy"(Atlantic) and Charles Johnson "Never Had A Love So Good" (Alston) among the best records that I ever discovered."

I remember talking to Richard Searling on the night of the swap deal with Sam, and he confessed to not being convinced that he had come out of the deal on top. Although the two '60s tracks were probably amongst the best dance records ever played at the Casino, Richard, like Sam, knew that records of the calibre of Larry Houston just had to be played, regardless of what decade they came from.

Of course, to a '60s junkie like me, it was great to hear Richard playing his new acquisitions. The Don Parker record – actually Damon Fox "Packin' Up" (Fairmount) – would have been a monster hit at any venue or in any era of the scene, it was undiluted, uptempo '60s soul. The Bobby Jason track, which turned out to be William Powell "Heartache Souvenirs" (Powerhouse) although not having the initial impact of "Packin' Up", still sounds as good now as it did in 1979, and features what I think is the best intro to any Northern Soul record. Remember that in the Mecca days, Levine and Curtis used to judge a record by the first thirty seconds!

Amongst the debris of ill-feeling and backbiting that was Wigan Casino in 1979, Richard Searling was the main reason that the soul faithful kept coming back each week. Paradoxically, just as the Casino hit an all time low as far as its legendary atmosphere was concerned, the standard of the new material being played reached its apex. Many people who were part of the scene in '79 are of the opinion that this was the best ever year for new '60s rare soul at the Casino. It was also the best year musically for converting rabid '60s only purists to the belief that, as Berry Gordy once vowed: "It's what's in the grooves that counts".

LEFT: *My preferred method of travel to the Casino – in the back of a Transit van full of women*
RIGHT: *The gorgeous, pouting Elaine Soley from Kidderminster, who helped me put these pictures together – at Casino Oldies in 1980.*

Richard's policy throughout the Casino years was simple and constant: play the best, screw the rest. No one could doubt the quality of a playlist like that, whether they be '60s or '70s soul inclined. Indeed, I would suggest that the material Richard was playing in '79 would stand comparison to the music of any other year, not only at the Casino, but any venue you care to name.

What made Richard's contribution even more extraordinary was that alongside those '60s gems, he also had a '70s playlist of equal quality, and his Saturday night spot would be a mixture of the best of both.

I realised that you couldn't slate a record just for the date on its label; the real quality of soul music is that it is timeless. Richard and Soul Sam were right to play stuff like Charles Johnson and Bobby Thurston for their soulful content, just as they were right to play Ike Strong and Roy Dawson for their dance floor appeal. Dave Godin's words rang true – Northern Soul did become stronger through change. Perhaps some of us would have done better to just enjoy the quality of the music, rather than make an issue of what we thought was best for the scene. Anyway, more of Richard's playlist later, but to get back to Sam, I asked him for his memories of Wigan, the good, the bad, and inevitably, the controversial...

"My lasting memories of Wigan are both good and bad. Good because it was the focal point of the scene for so long, because it transformed an underground scene into the monster that it still is today. There's no doubt that without the Casino, Northern Soul would have gone the same way as the punk scene, but this one venue held such magic that even now, this many years after its closure, it still holds a fascination."

Sam believes, however, that Wigan's success was also its downfall; to be so successful it had to rely on commercial interests, sometimes to the exclusion of the basic principals upon which the Northern scene was built. "As the biggest venue for so long, the Casino also had the biggest responsibility for the progression of the scene and its music. Unfortunately, it was the over-commercialisation of Wigan Casino that hampered the development of Northern Soul."

It would take several chapters to list all of Sam's discoveries, so what were his own favourites over the years?

"I would have to include Moses Smith, and other obvious ones would be Gwen Owens and Little Joe Cook from the Cleethorpes days.

RICHARD'S MODERN SOUL PLAYLIST INCLUDED:

Larry Houston	"Let's Spend Some Time Together"	(HMFP)
	(c/u Top Cat)	
C. B. Overton	"Superstar Lady"	(Shock)
J. B. Moore	"I Don't Ever Break That Rule"	
The Pages	"Heartaches And Pain"	(Sunstruck)
	(c/u Emotions)	
Z. Z. & Co.	"Gettin' Ready For The Get Down"	(Columbus)
Roy Dawson	"Over The Top"	(Coemands)
	(c/u Chicago Gangsters)	
Alfie Davidson	"Love Is A Serious Business"	(Mercury)
Ike Strong	"Your Love Keeps Me Dancing"	(Noble)
	(c/u Lee Moore)	
Curtis	"How Can I Tell Her?"	(Charm City)
Bobby Thurston	"Just Ask Me"	(Mainline)
Will Collins & Willpower	"Is There Anything I Can Do"	(Bareback)
	(c/u Love Committee "Just Call My Name")	
Charles Johnson	"Never Had A Love So Good"	(Alston)

the Twans of course, and modern stuff like Prince Phillip Mitchell and Charles Johnson. The best bit of business I ever did was to buy Gwen Owens, Little Joe Cook and the Sequins "Try My Love" all on the same day for £60. Not a bad investment, that!"

Being at the sharp end of the scene throughout the '70s, I wondered if he had any regrets?

"I regret dropping '60s material in 1979. I was wrong to say that '60s soul was dead. I also regret my part in the divisions which split the scene back then...I think in hindsight we should all have followed Richard's lead and played '60s and '70s together, as both had an important role to play."

Some of the people who slated Sam for his '70s only policy at the Casino should remember that before his about-face on '60s, he was the only DJ who came close to matching Richard for the quality of his playlist, classic Casino records like Damon Fox, William Powell, and the Cashmeres all originated from him, not to mention what is regarded by some to be the best instrumental ever played on the scene, the Dogs' "Soul Step".

As a footnote to my tribute to Soul Sam, this story says more about the dedication which he has given the scene than any of my ramblings. On 8th May, 1998, I was chatting to Sam at a soul night at the Lea Manor Hotel near Wolverhampton. He was browsing through a few sale boxes when a guy came along with four records and gave them to Sam with a view to making a sale. They were:

- The Sharpets "Lost In The World Of A Dream" (Sound City) £250
- 7th Avenue Aviators "Should O' Held On" (Congress-demo) £150
- The Construction "Hey Little Way Out Girl" (Sync 6) £250
- Al Williams "I Am Nothing"(La Beat) £500

Sam examined the Al Williams record, and finding it to be in mint condition, as it was in 1967 when brand new, he nonchalantly asked the guy if he would take a cheque, as he didn't have 500 quid in his back pocket. The guy said he would, and Sam duly obliged. Pure class.

Over the years, Soul Sam's contribution to the development of Northern Soul has been of paramount importance, and his love for the music is still as strong today as it has ever been. He has always been, and will always remain, one of the true gentlemen of our scene.

Chapter Seven "LISTEN TO THOSE MEMORIES"

IN ANY WALK of life there will always be those who refuse to change with the times; secure in the belief that their particular opinion is the only sensible one. They live in a world of cosy remembrance, sheltered from the inevitable reality of change by their love of a bygone era. On the Northern Soul scene, the presence of such people almost destroyed the whole movement.

Northern Soul has got to be the most fragmented, factional and sub-divided musical scene that has ever existed, much less grown into a major musical cult of thirty years standing! We took records from the sixties which no one had ever heard, and played them to a discerning cross-section of youth in the seventies who were sick and tired of the records that everyone had heard. In so doing, we created an insatiable market for something that could not be obtained anywhere else, and made stars of Black American artists who had been ignored in their own country a decade before.

Small wonder then that the music industry and media felt compelled to try to cash-in on the trend. It must have felt so threatened by Northern Soul when it discovered that it would not 'sit up and beg' in the same way as disco. To the outsider, the whole concept of our scene was bizarre, travelling hundreds of miles to dance all night to anonymous music and revelling in our own elitist sub-culture. There was clearly something dark and sinister about our lifestyle.

And yet, despite its differing factions and sub-divisions, Northern Soul remains the simplest, most uncommercial, and most completely rewarding music that there could be. There are no 'World Tours' to be flogged to death by banal media publicity, no gimmicks, no 'hard-sell'. Just a venue, a promoter, a group of DJs, a crowd and a dance floor, and that is the way it has always been. Yes, the faces and the sounds changed but the format and the values did not. On a basic level, you could say that, you took out as much as you were prepared to put in. If all you required from a visit to Wigan was to see friends and have a dance, then the arguments about musical direction probably went right over your head. If on the other hand you had a genuine love for the music, and a desire to see it progress, then chances are that you would have found yourself embroiled in a few heated exchanges now and then. I don't think that there was any such animal as a 'typical' soul fan during the Casino years, or even today for that matter. Some would only be interested in hearing the latest spins of the top jocks, some would dance to whatever was on the turntable at the time, some didn't give a toss either way, because they spent the night in the record bar buying and trading rare tracks. On the other hand, some were only interested in oldies. I knew quite a few people who only went to Wigan for Mr M's oldies room.

The oldies were a scene within a scene. There were various categories of oldie, some of which could be grouped together by the labels on which they had originally been recorded, such as Stax, Atlantic or Motown. Then there were records which had been played first at a particular club, and thus evoked memories of that particular era, such as the Torch, Twisted Wheel, Catacombs or Blackpool Mecca.

Allied to this, oldies were what the collectors were buying and selling in the record bar, as very few of the top sounds ever became available to the average collector. Harpo, Carl Jones, myself, and one or two other Wolverhampton lads had good collections on which we spent a lot of money each week, but we were not in the same league as the record dealers like Dave Withers from Manchester or Tim Ashibende from Stoke. They were the only people who could realistically get hold of any of the really big current sounds.

So as you can see, oldies were a very big part of the scene, even to those of us who preferred to listen and dance to the current big sounds of the day. At one time or another, even the most over-played oldie was a top sound, and those who remembered it being played for the first time would always have special memories come flooding back, however often it was played. Thus, as well as the top DJs like Russ, Richard, Pep, Alan Rhodes and others whose job it was to find and break new material, the Casino also catered for those who preferred older material with a line up of specialist oldies DJs, who not only worked in Mr M's, but also in the main room.

Up until 1976, the main room policy was seven hours of new material, with Dave Evison supplying an oldies hour between 7am and the end of the all-night session. With Mr M's as a separate oldies only room from 1974, this made the equation thus: main room seven hours of newies, Mr M's' four hours plus one hour in the main room equalled

Mr. M's . . . The Oldie Goldie

session was opened. A non-stop selection of OLDIES were played, I don't believe anyone even spoke over the mic, that night, and for five glorious hours Brian and Alan along with the help of Kenny Spence, Mike Rolo, Steve Whittle, plus a whole host of helpers, ran the thing perfectly. The crowd of course were fascinated with the whole event, for the first time in two years, they were allowed beyond those two metal doors, and at one point during the night, I would honestly say that there were more people in M's than in the main hall. The first night to all intents and purposes should have been the last, but such was the response in successive weeks for this 'new' room to be opened again that the petition with over 1000 names, finally convinced us that M's was HERE TO STAY. Gerry I'm pleased to say was more than happy about the decor after the first session and with accurate timing and organisation, we were able to continue clearing the Cabaret crowds, and re-open approximately 60 minutes later as an Oldie's room. Such has been the demand for 'Oldies' that through the success of M's, the first Friday and mid-month Allnighter sessions came into being, and no one can say that these have not been a tremendous success.

I must admit that in the early days, our newer, and less qualified Jocks were given their first work in the oldies room, but without a doubt these days, the guys who spin in M's are as well respected as any other on the scene.

Our established tried and tested line up at the moment is as follows.

KENNY SPENCE

Kenny is the Jock in charge of proceedings in M's, he is the guy who organises spots, is responsible for equipment, and generally keeps the rest of the guys together. He really does do an incredible job, and since he has been involved in one way or another with the Casino for as long as I can remember, must rate as the longest serving Jock on our books. During the day Kenny works at the Horwich Loco Works and must be the only fella I know who has actually built his very own 'Soul Train'.

BRIAN RAE

Brian is our all purpose Jock, working in both rooms, and guaranteed to work anytime, anywhere, anyplace . . . he must be the most well travelled DJ in the country, I have known him to be at one end of the country in the morning, work two gigs during the afternoon, do a spot in the north of Scotland in the evening and still get to an Allnighter at Wigan to work both halls. His selection of oldies is second to none, probably due to the fact that he bought them when they were 'first' issued. Brian is a full time Jock, and lives in Warrington.

STUART BRACKENRIDGE

Alias the taller half of the now defunct 'Soul Brothers'. Stuart has been in M's almost from the start and has the reputation of being one of the nicest guys on the scene. He has an incredible knowledge of sounds, and I have never yet seen him play to anything less that a full floor. Stuart is in fact a highly qualified 'chef' during the day, and is noted for his 'Sliced Tomato' and 'Green Onion' dishes. (Sorry Stuart). He lives in Horwich, near Bolton.

STEVE WHITTLE

Steve I remember was at the very first Casino Allnighter, he was one of our regular customers, and was in fact among the few who insisted that we should try Allnighters at the Casino in the first place. Steve was also one of the first Jocks to work in M's, and I remember him helping out on the first night during the

2nd Anniversary. With the exception of a very short break when he got married, Steve has been with us throughout, and is a very essential part of the team. A landscape gardener by day, Steve really does 'Dig' his music.

A trip down Memory Lane for Mr M's fans which was printed in the 7th anniversary edition of the Casino's own mag Northern Noise.
Brian and Steve are still deejaying at various venues throughout the country, although tragically Kenny died shortly after the club's closure. Stuart made a guest appearance at the 25th anniversary bash at Wigan's Maxime's in 1998.

five hours of oldies. A good balance, and one that reflected the importance given to unearthing new material in those early days.

However, in February 1976 the Casino began its monthly oldies all-nighters on the first Friday of each month thereafter. As already stated, these were a phenomenal success, so much so that some regulars to the Saturday all-nighter began to miss the odd night. Instead of four all-nighters per month, they would attend two or three Saturdays plus the Friday oldies. That is when the attendances began to fall more dramatically.

The punters were dropping new material for oldies. This may have been bad news for the scene's progression, but to owner Gerry Marshall it was worrying financially; instead of four full houses each month he was now getting one packed night and four with average attendances which were dropping each month. So it was decided by the management that the regular Saturday night would begin to programme more oldies in an attempt to woo back those people who had been lost to the Friday all-nighter, thus more and more oldies replaced new sounds in the main room.

Alongside Dave Evison's spot came Mr M's DJs Brian Rae and Steve Whittle, who alternately provided the 6am to 7am slot. Russ too, in his prime-time spot of midnight to 2am began to include more oldies. The net result was that the equation had changed dramatically: from a twelve hour all-nighter, (eight hours main room, four hours Mr M's) it was now eight hours of oldies and four hours newies. Wigan Casino was on the road to ruin. Steve Whittle, veteran of almost every Casino all-nighter agrees: "It may seem strange coming from an oldies DJ, but I firmly believe that the Friday all-nighter was the start of the Casino's demise. Then again, as the end took five-and-a-half years to come around, we must have been doing something right!"

Born and bred in the town, Steve witnessed the entire Casino story at firsthand, and remembers the days before the all-nighters began. "I was a regular at the Emp from about 1971 and I saw loads of top soul acts there: the Tams, Major Lance, Edwin Starr, Arthur Conley, Jimmy Ruffin and Chairmen Of The Board. We knew in June of '73 that the all-nighters were coming, mainly because the Torch had closed down in March of that year. I had been to about 15-20 all-nighters at the Torch and Va-Va's in Bolton, so I suppose you could call me a fan by that time."

Steve also recalls how the town found the prospect of having kids invade each Saturday night rather hard to get used to. "When the all-nighters first started, they ran from 2am until 8am. But Station Road would be chock-full of people from about midnight onwards, making it impossible for traffic to get through. Eventually, the police complained to the management, and the problem was eased by opening up the Beechcomber cafe, which was in the same building as the Casino, from 12 'til 2am, and again in the morning from 8am 'til 10, to get the people off the street. Kenny Spence put some decks in there, and four of us, Kenny, Brian Rigby, Allan Cain and myself did the DJing for free."

Some problems surrounding the Casino's early days were not so easily dealt with, however: "For the first year or so, the nighters were very controversial, and the local people made it clear that they didn't want them to continue. It was particularly bad if the local papers covered a court case involving drugs. Naturally, everyone who went to the Casino was tarred with the same brush. As time wore on, the all-nighter became accepted, if not welcomed by the locals, but really, it was a lot of fuss for just six hours a week! Without all the stuff in the papers, most of the Borough would never have known about the all-nighters, much less worried about them!"

Steve was also present at the birth of Mr M's; a happy accident which almost didn't happen. "On the night of the first anniversary, there were so many people on the streets outside the club without tickets again, that the police complained to the management. Gerry Marshall who owned the club decided to open the small, recently refurbished cabaret club at the back of the main building to ease the congestion. This was only ever meant to be a one-off occasion, just an emergency measure. The club was named after Gerry, and that's how Mr M's first started."

The problem was, that M's had been open for its usual Saturday night business and there was a lot of work to be done very quickly to make it usable as a disco. "The cabaret had been on until 2am, and when the regulars left, there were glasses to be collected, the room to be swept out and all the gear from down in the Beachcomber to be brought in and set up. That's besides the 70 or 80 tables, each with four chairs, to be shifted into the corridor, the bar to be restocked with soft drinks, and the three large carpets to be rolled up and carried out so that we could get at the dance floor!"

By some miracle, everything was ready by 2.55am. At 3am, the black doors which joined M's to the balcony of the main room were opened.

WIGAN CASINO ALL~NIGHTER

VISIT THE HEART OF SOUL
Every Sat. Night/Sun Morning Midnight-8am

FEATURING THE COUNTRY'S NO. 1 SOUL SPINNERS

RUSS WINSTANLEY & RICHARD SEARLING

Plus Top regular Guest D.J.s KEITH MINSHULL, BRIAN RAE, SOUL SAM, PAT BRADY, DAVE EVISON etc. and other top guest soul spinners. (Featuring two floors with KENNY SPENCE, BRIAN, STUART & GAL in Mr. M's playing THE OLDIES) ● NORTHERN SOUL nights every Wednesday (7.30-11 p.m.) and Friday (7.30-11 p.m.) ● Featuring RUSS & STUART (NO MEMBERSHIP REQUIRED).

The Big One!
Friday/Saturday Morning   12 Midnight to 8a.m.

FEBRUARY 1st
"Come and listen to those memories"

4th ANNIVERSARY
OLDIES ALLNIGHTER
(would you believe it!)
8 NON-STOP HOURS OF OLDIES ON TWO FLOORS, FEATURING ALL THE TOP REGULAR OLDIES SUPER-SPINNERS, PLUS LOTS OF GUESTS.

100's SPECIAL BIRTHDAY PRESENTS TO BE GIVEN AWAY
PLUS EVERY PERSON WILL RECEIVE SPECIALLY EMBROIDERED ANNIVERSARY BADGE
FREE ON THE NIGHT!

ADVANCE TICKETS £3.50 each
(MEMBERS ONLY)
SEND P.O.'s ONLY and S.A.E.

Be early - Everyones Comin!

TO BECOME A MEMBER YOU MUST BE OVER 18
— MEMBERSHIP IS NOW 25p
Applications to arrive 48 hrs before you do.
Please send SAE

Wigan Casino Soul Club. Station Road, Wigan, WN1 1YQ. Lancashire W.C.S.C. application form for membership . . .

I (name)

of (address)

Do apply for membership to Wigan Casino Soul Club. I am over 18 years of age and agree to abide by the rules of the Club.

I had so many wonderful nights at the Casino that it's almost impossible to pick one out as the best, but if pushed I'd have to say February 1st, 1980. The 4th anniversary of the Oldies 'nighters really was a night to remember!

"Within five minutes, we were totally packed out! The four of us who worked the Beachcomber did the DJing, with one or two spots from the main room staff as well. We actually got paid for that one!"

Mr M's quickly gained a special atmosphere of its own, and following that first night, literally hundreds of people went knocking at Gerry Marshall's door to ask that it become a regular feature of the all-nighters. "There were petitions handed in to the managers' office, 'phone calls, even threats made to boycott the place, but Gerry's answer to all of them was 'No!' Eventually, maybe for a bit of peace and quiet Gerry caved in. More cynically, perhaps the reason was purely financial. The capacity would be 500 extra, the admission price would go up by £1 to cover the cost of running both rooms, that's 500 quid, less the DJ bill of £32, a net gain of £468 per week. A bloody fortune in 1974!" Gerry Marshall's gain was also the Casino regulars' gain; Mr M's opened at 3am every week from then on, and its weekly four-hour oldies show became part of the Wigan Casino legend.

On the Casino's commercial outings, Steve has mixed thoughts: "We all wanted it to succeed and to continue as long as possible, but a consequence was that it became a focal point for the media, who all wanted a story. The media brought a lot of unwanted elements with it, but you have to ask yourself if the Casino would have been as big as it was if there had been no Disco Demand and no TV documentary. I don't think so."

Of those two ventures, the Granada TV documentary *This England* gave rise to strong feelings amongst the Casino faithful, as Steve recalls: "The TV show was a bad decision on the management's part, they went back on their word not to let the cameras in. I remember Mike Walker getting on stage and interrupting the DJ to talk to the crowd. He told us what the TV company wanted to do, and then said that Wigan Casino belonged to us, so we, the members would have the last word as to whether or not the cameras came. On a show of hands it was rejected almost unanimously, and Mike said, 'OK then, that's it – they don't come and that's that'. Those were his exact words. Two weeks later, they came and filmed. A lot of people boycotted that night, and there was real anger for a while. The cameras did attract a load of Mecca freaks in bin-liners and plastic sandals though, so that was a good laugh!"

Steve has equally strong views about the 1979 Casino Classics: "It was bloody awful. Rubbish is a polite term for the second-rate cover versions and sub-standard dross that they issued as "Classics from the Casino". Being totally honest, all I felt was embarrassment as a Casino DJ, being given free demos of "The Theme From Joe 90" and asked to play them in my spot." Being totally honest is one thing that Steve Whittle has always been and will always be respected for. Straight talking Lancastrians very seldom refer to a spade as anything other than a spade.

The diversity of the DJ line up over the eight years of the Casino's life gave rise to much debate and discussion among the punters on the subject of who played the best music. Of course, someone who didn't like newies would not champion Richard Searling, just as someone who didn't like oldies would not put Brian Rae's name forward for the title. It was this multi-opinion melting pot mentality that made the Casino years so engrossing to those of us who lived it and loved it. Steve: "My favourite DJ over the eight years was Richard, although Russ was brilliant from '73-'75 when he was getting Soussan's best new material. As for oldies jocks, it was always a pleasure for me to listen to Martyn Ellis, the first DJ to play oldies at Wigan. He did a 25 minute spot in the early days, which ran from 7.15 to 7.40 in the morning. Basically, Martyn was a total nutter. He never brought any records with him, and ten minutes before his spot he would be running around backstage shouting 'Whose records can I borrow then?' But he always managed to do a brilliant spot; outrageous, daring, funny, but always so professional. For my money, Martyn was the best 'Disc-Jockey' in the real sense of the word ever to play the all-nighter scene, as opposed to the rest of us who are just music specialists or serious collectors. He never lost sight of where he came from, the dance floor like the rest of us. I have always tried to keep those attributes with me in my DJ career, and if I've given people half of the pleasure Martyn Ellis gave me, I'll die a happy man."

February 1976 saw the start of a new venture for the Casino, the Oldies all-nighter. There were some who felt that this was yet another attempt to cash-in by the management, but there can be no denying the success of the idea. The lurid orange and yellow posters on the walls at the main entrance doors carried slogans like 'Come And Get These Memories' and featured the names of earlier Northern Soul clubs.

On the first Friday of each month, there was no debate between '60s and '70s fans, and all of the DJs became oldies DJs. The normal Saturday attendance was at least doubled, sometimes almost trebled.

Another picture tinged with sadness. On the balcony at Stafford's Top Of The World All-nighter in 1985 with 'Mad' Mick Davis and Penny 'Fish' Fisher from Kidderminster. Sadly, Penny died the following year.

The only way to dance at an oldies nighter was to be at the front of the queue and be first on the floor at opening time. You might manage ten or fifteen minutes before the floor became grid-locked with twelve or thirteen hundred bodies.

Oldies all-nighters were too packed. Christ only knows what would have happened if there had been a fire. They were too hot, opening the double doors at the main entrance was like opening a blast furnace. Sweat would drip off the end of your nose just standing still. There was nowhere to sit, it was a waste of time trying to check your bag into the cloakroom because the queue went almost the length of the balcony. Wherever you stood to chat, you were in someone's way, and the queue for the drinks bar resembled the beach at Dunkirk. In my entire life, I have never, and will never again, experience anything closer to heaven than an Oldies all-nighter at Wigan Casino.

We used to arrive between 12.30 and 1am on the coach which ran from Kidderminster and Redditch. The Wolverhampton crowd would be picked up at junction 10 of the M6 motorway: 15-20 of us in a group, trying to look inconspicuous. If I got inside at 1am, I would still be saying hello to people at 3.30am. I kid you not.

I have a hundred special memories of the oldies all-nighters, but only room to write about two of them, both of which happened on the same night, the fourth anniversary of the Friday sessions in February, 1980.

Gamber – Steve Clayton from Redditch – and I, had been asked by the regular coach organiser to collect the fares from the passengers, and pay the driver in his absence. This sounded like a good laugh, so we agreed. I went to Kidderminster, the coach's first pick-up point, straight from work on the Friday afternoon, and was met on the train station by Ian 'Wally' Wallace, and his gorgeous girlfriend Caroline.

After a few drinks in the Railway Tavern with the Kiddy soul set, we were picked up by the coach, which was empty except for Gamber. He told me that the guy who usually ran the coach had promised everyone that we would sort out the anniversary tickets in advance for the entire coach. All they had to do was give us the money and we would do the rest. You may recall my previous experience with anniversary tickets in 1975.

Gamber was not pleased. "What we gonna do, chap? This is a fifty-two-seater bus and we've got sixty seven on. Where the f— we gonna find sixty seven anniversary tickets from?"

"Do what we always do" I replied. "Panic like f— and hope something will turn up."

We made the usual pick-up in Redditch at the Sporran pub. As they boarded the coach, everyone thrust five and ten pound notes into our hands, confident that we would be giving them tickets in return. I can't remember which of us had the idea, but we decided to ring the Casino from our usual motorway stop at Sandbach services. I got through at the twentieth attempt and spoke to Doris Woods on reception. If you ever went to Wigan, you met Doris. She took your money on the door.

A night to remember…on board the anniversary coach, February 1980. Gamber from Redditch (my right) and I plan how to get hold of sixty seven anniversary tickets…

I asked if they could reserve 67 tickets on the door for our party, which we would pay cash for on our arrival, fully expecting the answer "Don't be so bloody stupid". To my amazement, she said yes, no problem, and took my name. Sorted. No sweat, mate. Me and Gamber have got it sussed. When we arrived at the Casino, we asked everyone to stay on the coach while we went to collect the tickets, which we did, armed with over two hundred quid in ten, five and one pound notes. What we completely forgot was the world famous queue/rugby scrum to get in, and it took us nearly twenty minutes to convince the bouncers that we had to get our reserved tickets from reception. Eventually, we made it, and we duly put the screwed up currency onto the cash desk and counted out the correct money for our 67 tickets. Doris thanked us, we thanked Doris and headed for the door, back to the coach.

"Oi!!! Where the bleedin' hell do you think you're going?" came the voice from behind us. "Back to the coach." said Gamber.

"Get up them stairs and stop blocking this f—— doorway! There's no passouts 'til three!"

So it came to pass that 65 people sat on the coach, thinking that we had done a runner, while Gamber and I tried to explain to the bouncers that the tickets we had just bought were as much use as tits on a bull if we could not give them to the people who had paid for them. When we finally got back to the coach it was almost 2am, and the 65 were discussing how best to dispose of our bodies after they had beaten us to death. Happy days.

The best, however, was yet to come. At that time I was going out with a girl called Gabby from Bangor in North Wales. Even though we only met at the Casino, we had become very close. Perhaps because we had a shared dedication to the scene and the Casino, or perhaps we were just two nineteen-year-olds who knew that life would never get any better than this. Or perhaps it was because she had such a fantastic bum. Who knows.

We had arranged to meet outside the building as we always did, at about 1am, but I was otherwise engaged at that time. When I finally got into the main room, Richard was just starting his spot. He played, amongst others, Larry Laster's "Go For Yourself" (Loma), Joe Matthews' "Ain't Nothing You Can Do" (Kool Kat) and Life's "Tell Me Why" (Reprise). When confronted with a spot of that quality, whilst in the vicinity of a dance floor, I danced. The only space on the floor was at the stage end of the room, underneath the ultra-violet strip lights, that made your skin look deeply tanned and made a white t-shirt glow in the dark. So there I stayed for about half an hour.

As the standard of the records in Richard's spot got even better, I just kept on dancing; it would have been a crime to leave the floor with such superb oldies as Lee Andrews' "I've Had It" (Crimson), Billy Woods' "Let Me Make You Happy" (Sussex), The Apollas' "Mr. Creator" (Warner Brothers) and Jock Mitchell's "Not A Chance In A Million" (Impact) on the turntables.

It was customary for the dancers to applaud each record as it ended, to show not only appreciation for the individual records, but also thanks to the DJ for playing it. That may sound weird to anyone whose only experience of discos is the local Tiffany's or Locarno, but it was as natural as breathing to a Casino crowd. At the end of one record, about an hour into his spot, I applauded along with everyone else, then stood waiting for Richard to introduce the next goodie. Will it be The Volcanos? Or Mel Williams? Or even The Ivories or The Vonettes? Suddenly, two arms wrapped themselves around my waist from behind me, and a familiar face appeared on my shoulder, wearing a familiar smile.

"One o'clock, he said. Usual place, he said. Don't be late, he said…" I turned around and there was Gabby, looking more beautiful than ever. How could I possibly have forgotten that I was supposed to meet her over two hours ago?

"Oh, it's terrible sorry that I am! I'm an awful man, isn't it?" I said in a naff Welsh accent. Then, remembering that the following Monday was a Bank Holiday, I asked her if she would come back to Wolverhampton for the weekend to make up for only seeing each other for five hours that night. She said she would love to, and gave me a big smile. I squeezed her as though we had been apart for seven years, not days. It was pure magic. It was perfect. The Casino was packed to the rafters with hundreds of friends, the music was pure quality soul, and me and Gabs had the whole weekend together to look forward to. Life just didn't get any better than that weekend.

Mushy, you cry? Perhaps. Sentimental? You bet your ass! You can't recall something as good as that night without sounding a little like the latest Mills and Boon. If you were to hold a gun to my head, I think that I would have to choose that night, as being the best that I can ever remember at the Casino, and that, believe me, is praise indeed. But as we all know, real life is not like Mills & Boon, and Gabby and I went our separate ways before the Casino closed down. Teenage love doesn't last forever, only the memory of it does. But in the words of the song, I still remember the feeling, and I always will. God bless you Gabs, wherever you are.

On nights like that one, I can remember some of the older faces (people of thirty-plus) saying things like "This is almost as good as the Torch" or, "Tonight is like being back at the Twisted Wheel". That used to annoy me because it was as if they were saying, "Yes, we can see how good the Casino is, but our era was better." These were usually the same people who slated the club in its early days, either for its non-exclusive musical policy, such as playing records that had been discovered at other clubs or its commercial ventures like Disco Demand and *Top Of The Pops*.

I was not old enough to have visited the Wheel or the Torch, but nobody will ever convince me that either of those venues was better than, or even as good, as the Casino at its best.

None of the clubs whose names are revered by their former patrons ever achieved their 'legendary' status until after they had closed, or had been closed down, regardless of how many top sounds had originated at them.

Wigan Casino, on the other hand, enjoyed world-wide fame during its lifetime: the US music bible *Billboard* reported in 1977 that the club was the best disco in the world, with Studio 54 running a close second! To hold an all-nighter every weekend, sometimes two, for over eight years was a fantastic achievement, and to maintain such a high standard of original records over those years proves the point. No venue on the all-nighter scene ever had the impact or one tenth of the staying power of the Casino. If that doesn't cause a row at my next all-nighter, nothing will!

It is true to say that the advent of the oldies nights started a two-tiered scene as far as the Casino was

"Mr Oldies" himself, Uncle Brian Rae!

concerned, and this was exacerbated by the further addition of the 'mid-monthly oldies specials', in the late seventies.

These all-nighters went out on the second or third Friday of the month, and were billed as being in response to the 'incredible demand' of the regular sessions on the first Friday of the month. Predictably, some on the newies side of the two-tiered system again cried rip-off.

These nights did, however, cater for a more specialist punter. One night was given the title of 'The Motown All-Nighter', at which the DJs played predominately Motown records. If you think that policy was a bit restrictive, you only have to consider the massive volume of material that came under the Detroit giant's umbrella. For every hit record that the label produced, they made another ten that were not hits. Also, whereas at any one time, there was only one output for their records in this country, in the USA they had a multitude of labels: Tamla, Motown, VIP, Gordy, Soul, to name but a few.

Another special was the 'Mod All-Nighter' in 1979, to cater for those who had seen the film *Quadrophenia*, and liked to dress-up in ridiculous clothing bought from Oxfam shops. I did not attend that night, so cannot comment upon its musical content, however, the more astute reader will have already guessed that this was probably not one of the Casino's finer moments. Although these mid-month sessions did not gain much in the way of crowd co-operation, the regular oldies continued to hold the fascination of both the young and old of the Northern Soul scene, either socially or on the dance floor.

Oldies nighters were fascinating times for record collectors, too. The record bar would be absolutely packed with sale boxes of all sizes. Some dealers would only bother to attend an oldies once a month, rather than set up their sale boxes at the less well attended Saturday nights.

Brian Rae once told me that Gerry Marshall had gone mad when he overheard one dealer telling his friend that he had made over £300 at one Friday session. For a few

Straight up the stairs, please!!!
Left to right: Jo, Caroline and Wally from Kidderminster climb the stairs to heaven.

Utopia…the 'Heart of Soul', packed to the rafters for the fourth oldies anniversary.

weeks after that, the management issued rules to limit the amount of records that could be brought into the Casino for sale; the large DJ boxes which held 250 to 300 singles were banned, and only the small square boxes with a capacity of 50 singles, were allowed into the record bar. Gerry, being first and foremost a business man, obviously took exception to anyone making money in his club if he was not in on the deal.

Another aspect of having all the DJs playing oldies was that it was possible to see some of the rarest records ever, from the collections of the top jocks like Richard, Russ and Keith Minshull. These DJs were of course playing new material at the Saturday all-nighter, not oldies. Therefore, what they put onto the decks was usually either on an unknown label, or covered up, so it was great for label-lookers like me to see what these jocks had in their oldies boxes.

A classic example was Richard's. His box for the oldies nights was like an Aladdin's cave, and I can remember just standing and watching as he pulled out one rare gem after another during his spot. One of the oddities of rare soul is that some of the records were released on more than one label, and the value of such a record would quadruple, if you could find a copy on the less well-known or local label. Richard had a copy, the only copy I believe, of Nolan Chance "Just Like The Weather" on a small Chicago label, Bunky. The less rare copies were on the Constellation label, and would sell for less than £20. One collector once

92

wrote that he was in the record bar at one oldies, when Richard played the Nolan Chance record. Suddenly filled with a desire to own the Bunky copy, he rushed up to the stage and offered Richard the princely sum of £100 for it, which was politely refused.

Non-collectors would say that it doesn't matter what label a record is on, it sounds just the same whether it is the £100 original or a £1.25 pressing. Try telling that to a dedicated collector and you would receive a less than polite answer. Someone once said that buying a re-issue or a pressing when you wanted the original was like buying glass when you wanted a diamond. I couldn't put it any better than that.

To collectors like Harpo and me, the oldies nighters provided the best opportunity to get hold of that elusive sound to add to our collections. This is a list of records that I can remember either having bought myself, or seen for sale at the Friday all-nighter.

- Tamiko Jones "I'm Spellbound" (Golden World-yellow issue) £125
- Jimmy Mack "My World Is On Fire" (Palmer) £60
- Freddie Chavez "They'll Never Know Why" (Look-blue issue) £70
- Patti & The Emblems "I'm Gonna Love You A Long, Long Time" (Kapp-black issue) £60
- Williams & Watson "Too Late" (Okeh-white demo) £25
- Larry Atkins "Ain't That Love Enough" (Highland-white demo) £45
- Debbie Dean "Why Am I Loving You" (VIP-issue) £100
- Inspirations "Your Wish Is My Command" (Midas) £20
- Valentinos "Sweeter Than The Day Before" (Chess-white demo) £30
- Jimmy Fraser "Of Hopes And Dreams And Tombstones" (Columbia-white demo) £30
- Embers "Watch Out Girl" (MGM-yellow demo) £40
- Patrick Bradley "Just One More Chance" (Decca-pink demo) £45
- Four Perfections "I'm Not Strong Enough" (Party Time) £40
- RPM Generation "Rona's Theme" (Romar-black issue) £50
- Dean Courtney "I'll Always Need You" (RCA Victor-black issue) £60
- Donna King "Take Me Home" (Hot Line) £30
- Duke Browner "Crying Over You" (Impact-red issue) £35
- Stanley Mitchell "Get It Baby" (Dynamo-red issue) £60
- Silky Hargraves "Keep Loving Me Like You Do" (Dearborn-white demo) £20
- Jerry Fuller "Double Life" (Challenge-black issue) £50

LEFT: *A poignant picture – Cleo from Worcester poses with Gary Stubbs, also from Worcester and Phil Shelton from Wolverhampton, both of whom have since passed away. (May 1981)*
RIGHT: *From right to left, Gethro from Wolverhampton, Dave Evison, me, some bird walking by with two coffees. (Hinckley All-nighter, September 1982)*

I didn't buy them all myself, but if I had had the money, I would have done. It's hard to explain the attraction of spending so much money on records, and remember, the prices of the records listed are what they were selling for back in 1979-80, it just becomes such an obsession that the money you have to spend to get that prized item becomes irrelevant.

Another area of rare soul collecting, and one which really sorted the true collector from the less dedicated, concerned those who only bought records which were released on British labels. Mostly, these records had already been released on American labels, and the UK labels like Stateside, London, Stax and the British subsidiaries of Atlantic and Motown were the outlets in this country.

However, the prices of UK labels, especially pre-releases or demos, were sometimes two or three times higher than the US original. In particular though, Tamla-Motown and Stateside were the most collectable, with London and Atlantic also highly sought after.

Both the Tamla Motown and Stateside labels were distributed in this country by EMI Records, and the normal issues (not promo copies) featured a large '45 RPM' logo on the right-hand side of the label. The rarer pre-release copies, which were sent out to radio stations for advance promotion before the record's release date, were white instead of black, and featured a large red 'A' on the plug side. From about 1967 onwards, the demos of both labels changed to green, with a large white 'A'.

The London label's later colours were black and silver, and Atlantic issues were originally black then red. Demo copies of both the original London and Atlantic 45s were yellow. On these four labels alone you would find the majority of what UK collectors were looking for. Each of them had access to the releases of many US soul labels; for instance, Stateside's UK releases came from a diverse range of US labels including Musicor, Golden World, Swan, Amy, Mala, Bell, 20th Century, Constellation, Goldwax, ABC, Laurie, Vee-Jay and Diamond. Tamla-Motown drew upon the many aforementioned US subsidiaries of the Motown corporation.

Many of the UK labels in the '60s were pressed and distributed by the giant EMI company, and US labels such as Columbia and MGM used this outlet to access the UK market.

Motown records had started the UK market for US soul material with their early releases, which were leased to a variety of different labels. London, Fontana, Oriole and Stateside all had Motown songs in their catalogues. Berry Gordy being the astute man that he is, soon realised that the UK was not only a huge market in itself, but also the gateway to Europe, and in 1964 he launched his own product in this country.

Tamla-Motown records became the only label that released the US Motown hits from artists like the Supremes, the Four Tops, the Temptations, Martha & the Vandellas, Little Stevie Wonder, the Isley Brothers and Marvin Gaye to the UK market.

Darrell Banks recorded this classic Northern Soul side in 1966, and the record was released in the UK on Stateside 536. However, the record was first intended for release on the London label, until they cancelled the issue.

London had pressed the usual pre-release copies for distribution to radio stations, and as can be seen, a release date was set for August 19th, 1966.

Exactly why London decided to pull the plug on the record has been lost in the mists of time, but the yellow promotional copies, as opposed to the black stock issues, gained 'super rare' status amongst collectors.

This was reflected in the price that the serious collectors would pay to get hold of a copy of one of the records in the 'rare as rocking horse shit' category. An American Revilot copy would sell for about £10, and a Stateside UK copy for about the same, however, if you were fortunate enough to find a London promo, (as likely as finding the Shroud of Turin at a car boot sale) the owner would probably be asking for offers in excess of £100.

To the collectors of rare soul on UK labels, Tamla-Motown, Stateside, London, HMV, Columbia (later CBS records), Sue and Pye International represent the cream of the crop. These labels, like the Darrell Banks track on London, are always more sought after for their pre-release copies – a sort of status symbol for the serious collector to have in his box.

The following list illustrates the diversity of material that was released on the Stateside label; every one would be considered a Northern Soul classic, but the comparative prices of a Stateside copy and a US label copy of each record tell the real story behind collecting British labels. The prices given for each record are based on lists that were published from 1979 to 1981, and it is fair to assume that the dealers behind the lists would have visited the Casino's oldies all-nighters, as this was by far and away the number one night for business.

- Invitations "What's Wrong With Me Baby" (US DynoVoice) £10
  UK Stateside (Black issue) £15-£20
  UK Stateside (White demo) £50
- Gene Chandler "Nothing Can Stop Me" (US Constellation) £3
  UK Stateside (Black issue) £8
  UK Stateside (White demo) £30
- Reflections "Just Like Romeo & Juliet" (US Golden World) £3
  UK Stateside (Black issue) £5
  UK Stateside (White demo) £25

- Fascinations "Girls Are Out To Get You" (US Mayfield) £4
  UK Stateside (Black issue) £8
  UK Stateside (Green demo) £30
- Rufus Lumley "I'm Standing" (US Holton) £5
  UK Stateside (Black issue) £10
  UK Stateside (White demo) £60
- Incredibles "There's Nothing Else To Say" (US Audio Arts) £8
  UK Stateside (Black issue) £12
  UK Stateside (Green demo) £40
- Bob Kuban "The Cheater" (US Musicland USA) £6
  UK Stateside (Black issue) £8
  UK Stateside (White demo) £30
- Tams "Be Young, Be Foolish, Be Happy" (US ABC) £3
  UK Stateside (Black issue) £7
  UK Stateside (Green demo) £25
- Charlie Gracie "He'll Never Love You Like I Do"
  (US Diamond) £20
  UK Stateside (Black issue) £50
  UK Stateside (White demo) £100
- Darrell Banks "Open The Door To Your Heart"/
  "Our Love (Is In The Pocket)" (US Revilot) £10
  UK Stateside (Black issue) £12
  UK Stateside (White demo) £40
  (Also on yellow pre-release London label, never released in UK)
  £80-£100

For UK collectors however, it was the Tamla-Motown label which was prized above all others, and with a few exceptions, these were the most collectable of all British soul labels. The differences in the prices of the UK and US copies were staggering.

- Barbara McNair
  "You're Gonna Love My Baby"
  (US Motown) £8
  (UK issue) £20 (White demo) £60

- Kim Weston "Helpless"
  (US Gordy) £5
  (UK issue) £10 (White demo) £50
- The Miracles "Whole Lot Of
  Shaking" (US Tamla) £6
  (UK issue) £20
  (White demo) £60
- The Hit Pack "Never Say No
  To Your Baby" (US Soul) £10
  (UK issue) £20 (White demo) £70
- Isley Brothers "Why When Love Is
  Gone" (US Tamla) £5
  (UK issue) £12 (White demo) £50
- Brenda Holloway "Starting The Hurt All Over Again"
  (US Motown) £10
  (UK issue) £15 (White demo) £50
- The Supremes "He's All I Got" (US Motown) £10
  (UK issue) £12 (White demo) £60
- Chris Clark "From Head To Toe" (US V.I.P.) £8
  (UK issue) £20 (White demo) £50

Other collectable UK labels included Capitol, CBS, Pye International,
Cameo Parkway and HMV. Finding one could, however, test your bank
balance as well as your collecting instinct!

- Shane Martin "I Need You" (CBS demo) £70
- Lynn Randell "Stranger In My Arms" (CBS demo) £70
- Chapter Five "You Can't Mean It" (CBS demo) £50
- Alexander Patton "A Li'l Lovin' Sometimes" (Capitol demo) £50
- Chubby Checker "You Just Don't Know"
  (Cameo Parkway demo) £100
- Sapphires "Gotta Have Your Love" (HMV demo) £100
- Major Lance "Investigate" (Columbia demo) £50
- Jason Knight "Love Is Getting Stronger"
  (Pye International demo) £50
- Frankie & Johnny "I'll Hold You" (Decca demo) £50
- The American Poets "She Blew A Good Thing"
  (London demo) £60

Casino Oldies DJs on parade: Dave Evison (left) and Steve Whittle relax at an Oldies All-nighter.

The fact that the oldies dance floor was packed all night gave an opportunity for the DJs to experiment with more obscure and imaginative sounds – confident that there would not be a mass exodus by the dancers. Some of these less well-known records would then gain popularity, making them bigger as oldies than they had been when they were new sounds.

In that category were many records from Brian Rae's spot such as Youngblood Smith's "You Can Split" (Verve), Howard Guyton's "I Watched You Slowly Slip Away" (Verve), Levi Jackson's "This Beautiful Day" (Columbia) and Vala Regan's "Fireman" (Atlantic). To be honest, when these records did become favourites with the dancers, they became a pain in the neck, other jocks would receive requests for them, and you would hear the same record three or four times in a night, which in the case of "You Can Split", which I always hated anyway, was no laughing matter.

Of course, the DJs needed to have a definite direction in mind when playing oldies, just as they would when playing new material, otherwise the night would have consisted of eight hours of repetition with everyone playing Frank Beverly's "If That's What You Wanted" and the Del-Larks' "Job Opening" – classic examples of brilliant records which were systematically played to death.

Thus, the DJs tended to become known for playing their own material at the oldies nights as well as the newies nights, and everyone was happy; the dancers knew when their favourite sounds would be played, the DJs didn't have to play records which they didn't like, and the management presided over an ever growing success story.

It is widely accepted that the onset of the Oldies all-nighter signalled the beginning of the end for the Casino, as starved of the input of new material, the scene became stale and predictable. The oldies were certainly responsible for a dramatic drop in the regular Saturday attendance. When Alan Rhodes quit the scene altogether in early 1979, his spot was given to Soul Sam and Pat Brady on a fortnightly basis.

The oldies nighters were at their peak at that time, and depending on whose figures you believe, attendances were up to eighteen hundred people. The regular Saturday's patronage went down to six or seven hundred, even less on the Saturday following an oldies.

Soul Sam, for reasons explained earlier, did not DJ at a Wigan Oldies. He must have felt that the scene was disappearing up its own backside by actively encouraging fans to live in the past rather than look to the future. You have to sympathise with the logic behind that argument, but equally, you had to be present at an Oldies All-nighter to appreciate the pure, unbridled joy that they gave. The lives of everyone who experienced those nights will always be richer for having been there.

Steve Whittle: "Even though we used to complain that there were only six hundred in some Saturdays, how many other venues would get that many at all, never mind every week! The Casino became a victim of its own success; it re-wrote the record books every year, smashing attendance records in '73, '74, '75 and '76. So although 600 in the Casino was a decline in standards, it wasn't really all that bad, was it? Love them or loathe them, oldies are as much a part of the Northern Soul scene today as they were in the Casino years. And through them at the Oldies all-nighters, I had the best nights of my life. I honestly think that over the eight years, the Casino was as close to being perfect as it was possible to be, and the Friday Oldies nights were an experience you could never forget."

It is because of soul fans like Steve Whittle – with the scene running through their veins – that those nights will live forever.

STEVE WHITTLE'S TOP TEN PLAYLIST,
WIGAN OLDIES ALL-NIGHTER 1976-81 *(in no particular order!)*

Benny Spellman	"Fortune Teller"	(UK-London)
Earl Grant	"Hide Nor Hair"	(Decca)
Kelly Garrett	"Love's The Only Answer"	(Smash)
Stanley Mitchell	"Get It Baby"	(Dynamo)
Mel Williams	"Can It Be Me"	(Modern)
Thelma Houston	"Baby Mine"	(Capitol)
Gentlemen & Their Ladies	"Like Her"	(UK-Pye International)
Frank Beverly & The Butlers	"If That's What You Wanted"	(Sassy)
Edwin Starr	"Time"	(UK-Tamla-Motown)
Mr Flood's Party	"Compared To What"	(UK-Ember)

That then, was the oldies scene at Wigan Casino. From its solitary hour each week in the main room, it had grown, through the opening of Mr M's and the inception of the Friday Oldies all-nighter, into a much-loved 'sub-scene' to rival the traditional newies scene.

There was one Casino DJ however, who was not prepared to sit and watch the oldies scene take over completely. Richard Searling was getting ready for the get down…

Chapter Eight "ANOTHER SATURDAY NIGHT"

THE OLDIES ALL-NIGHTERS were in good shape. And those who only came to the Casino on the first Friday of the month went home happy. Unfortunately, for those of us who were required by addiction to attend the club five times per month, a healthy oldies scene meant that the newies scene suffered a sharp decline.

Added to the Mod invasion, the ever present debate on '60s and '70s soul, and the increased number of oldies that were being played on what was supposed to be newies night, in truth, nobody would have been surprised if the new rare soul scene had died out altogether in 1979, to be replaced by a purely oldies orientated scene. As I recall the more vocal of the '70s only brigade were forecasting just that.

Within this less than ideal scenario though, the newies scene did have something going for it. Pat Brady and Gary Rushbrook, who had joined the DJ staff with Soul Sam when Alan Rhodes retired from the scene, were unearthing and breaking some excellent new '60s records. And Richard Searling, who was already recognised as the country's top Northern DJ, with the help of John Anderson, began to introduce sounds that would turn the tide of opinion back towards rare soul.

Steve Whittle: "Richard brought credibility back to the Casino in 1979. It had been going through a really dross period with records like Muriel Day's "Nine Times Out Of Ten", a truly awful record, and James Coit's "Black Power", even worse than Muriel Day, and other fifth-rate crap. This period also coincided with the rise in popularity of the Yate all-nighter, and the older crowd voted with their feet."

Steve, like me, is a fan of Richard's superb playlist throughout the Casino years, so what does a veteran of almost every all-nighter believe was the turning point in 1979?

"Early in '79, Richard turned up two records that got people travelling back to the Casino: sounds that were so good that, like in the old days, the punters came to hear them because only he had them. One was the Christine Cooper cover up, (Vickie Baines "Country Girl") and the other was Joe Matthews."

Within every musical genre, a record comes along which does more than just bring back memories; it defines that particular style, that particular era, and everything that made it so special. Think of flower power, and "Let's Go To San Francisco" comes to mind. Punk rock and Johnny Rotten screeching "Pretty Vacant" might come back to haunt you. Ask a Casino regular of 1979 to choose an audio-time machine and my guess is he will choose, what was for me Richard's, and therefore Wigan Casino's, best ever record "I Don't Like To Lose", covered up as Joe Matthews.

In early 1979, Richard was guesting at a soul night at Wolverhampton's Wulfrun Hall. Amongst his other big plays of the time such as Chris Cerf's "Sweet Music" (Amy), Cheryl Ann's "I Can't Let Him" (Patty) and Gary Haines' "Keep On Going" (Sound), he played the record as a new spin.

The top DJs had the knack of knowing how much exposure to give to a new record in order to break it to the dance floor; too many plays of an average item would bore the crowd, the trick was to introduce it slowly amongst the proven floor-fillers. If it was good enough, it would gain interest and be requested. That night, I found my all-time favourite Northern Soul record.

The impact of "I Don't Like To Lose" however, was the equivalent of a pop record going straight to number one on the day of its release. Even staunch oldies fans were impressed and as the record took off, it crossed the barriers between old and new '60s fans. It was simply so good.

The collectors and the dealers went nuts to find out the record's true identity and over the next 12 months, it seemed to be the scene's major obsession. The label experts came up with various theories: it was an obscure West coast item, it was the Inserts, a missing number from the Kool Kat label, it was the Orchids, an unreleased track on Impact ...

Each week, people would march up to Richard armed with their latest idea, and he would smile and say "Try again next week, son!" For almost two years, it was the top sound in the country, and no one was any nearer to knowing the real identity of the artist than I had been back in the Wulfrun Hall.

It couldn't last forever though. By definition, a rare soul scene needs rare records, and the easiest way to preserve rarity is by anonymity. If this is lost, then so is exclusivity, and a large percentage of the hard work done by the DJ to break the record is wasted. The unwritten rule amongst the DJs of the scene therefore, was that if you obtain a record which is still covered up, you should cover your copy when you play it, respecting the work of the DJ who first discovered it. Never, but NEVER play it at any venue with the label uncovered to public scrutiny until it has been revealed by the original DJ who played it.

For reasons best known to himself, this is just what Kev Draper, a DJ at the Fleet all-nighter in Peterborough, did in 1980. Where he managed to get a copy of the record remains unclear, but at the following Saturday at Wigan, Richard was understandably less than amused. At the start of his spot, he said that he would not play the record again, and added: "It takes two years to make a record, and two minutes to destroy one. I sometimes wonder why we bother…"

1977 saw the debut of RCA's Grapevine label, a UK outlet for many of the previously unreleased records that had found popularity at Wigan. Unlike its contemporary, Casino Classics, it was regarded by most of the regulars to be more definitive of the true Casino sound, with releases such as Richard 'Popcorn' Wylie's "Rosemary, What Happened", Jimmy Burns' brilliant "I Really Love You" and the Agents classic "Trouble". The man in charge of the labels' output was none other than John Anderson.

Given the less than enthusiastic response to the Casino Classics venture, the purists could have been accused of being selective in their condemnation of the commercial side of Northern Soul when they received Grapevine releases with such interest. In total, there were forty-seven singles and three compilation albums released, most of which were available for the first time in the UK.

Also, with both John Anderson and Richard working for RCA, you could say that they had cornered the market with the Grapevine venture, as many of its titles were unearthed first by John and then made into dance floor favourites by Richard before their subsequent UK release. What cannot be denied is that the partnership between John and Richard gave the punters a reason to return to the Saturday newies nights, and gave the scene the best records it has ever had.

The following passage comes from a letter which I sent to Chris Fletcher's *Soul Source*, which he was kind enough to include in an issue in 1979.

"Finally can I say that having been a Casino regular for almost five years, the standard of the newies currently being played has never been better. This is due mainly to one man in my opinion, Richard Searling.

His playlist just keeps on getting better, and no one can argue that many of his discoveries would have been big at any venue, the Torch, the Wheel, the Catacombs etc.

Perhaps admiration might be thought of as too strong by some people, but Northern Soul is my life, and nobody gives me more pleasure through his music than R.S. Long may it continue!"

This was an opinion shared by other Casino DJs, Dave Evison once listed his favourite Wigan records as: "Anything Richard plays."

I asked Richard Searling for his memories of the collaboration with John Anderson, both as the benefactor of his major discoveries, and as colleagues at RCA Records.

"John was the source of practically all the records that I was fortunate enough to break, at both the Casino and other venues like the Ritz in Manchester. He is the person more than any other who brought soul into the UK which would otherwise not have been recognised – and his Grapevine label stands up even now as the only credible re-issue for them."

Logically then, Grapevine was the tangible conclusion for the work of both men in bringing those unknown tracks to the attention of the dancers?

"Certainly Grapevine was an obvious outlet for the massive amount of high quality soul that John was unearthing, from which the Casino definitely benefited. Some of the tracks he got from producers such as Weldon McDougal, Johnny Brantley and 'Popcorn' Wylie were previously unreleased even in the USA, so his label was the logical destination for such material – and I must add that RCA Records were very supportive of both John and myself."

Remembering that one of Richard's biggest records, "Hey Little Way Out Girl" was released on Grapevine under the cover-up identity of the 'Del Capris' rather than the true artists – the Construction – I asked him if Kev Draper's uncovering of "I Don't Like To Lose" as Cecil Washington spoiled a possible Grapevine release for the record.

"If he did, he'd never live it down would he? But you can rest easy, Kev, your Sherlock Holmes work made no difference one way or the other – the rights, to re-release the record, were unobtainable if I remember correctly!"

One of my most vivid memories of Richard's Casino spots was during the Casino Classics episode in early '79. Dave Evison and myself were with him on the stage and as he was nearing the end of his spot, Mike Walker appeared from behind the big gold curtains and asked if he had played any of the records which had been left in a pile beside the decks – all of which were on the Casino Classics label.

Richard explained that he didn't have enough time to play what he actually wanted to play, and Casino Classics tracks did not feature too highly on his preferred playlist. The upshot was that Richard took the pile of records and systematically played about thirty seconds of each one, giving each track an accompanying Radio One type introduction…

At the end of the performance as he put away his own records, Dave Evison said to him: "Well done son, I'm proud of you!!" As he left the stage, Richard turned and said: "I don't know if I'll see you next week – I might not have a job left!"

With this in mind, I asked Richard for his thoughts on the Casino Classics label, and how it compared to Grapevine and others in the same field.

"Unlike Grapevine, and even Pye's Disco Demand in '75, the label was aimed fairly and squarely at the 'new' Northern converts – punters who wanted a souvenir-style Wigan record. I can't recall coming under any specific management pressure to feature them – in fact I really liked Linda and the Funky Boys' first release for the label. As for the thirty-seconds-of-each-one incident, I had forgotten that! Just put it down to me being young and rather rebellious at the time – even Dave Godin once noted that I had a slightly volatile tendency!"

Despite the high profile that Richard had at the Casino, he was never one to get into heated debates with fellow DJs or punters, preferring instead to let the music do the talking. One of the few times that he did voice an opinion on the subject was in an article which appeared in *Northern Noise*:

"SIXTIES OR SEVENTIES?
What is all the fuss about?
Punters who don't like '70s music, DJs who don't rate the latest '60s 'discoveries' – it's all soul music isn't it?
New releases have always been played on this scene, some think it's wrong to do so, others think that they are on some sort of pioneering crusade by playing them!
Have they all got short memories?
Even back at the Wheel in Manchester, Freda Payne's "Band Of

Gold", R. B. Greaves' "Take A Letter Maria" and Chris Jackson's "I'll Never Forget You" were all played on the day of UK release, now people moan if any new US import is played! How can they fail to realise the brilliance of Phyllis Hyman's "You Know How To Love Me" or Skip Mahoney's "Janice"? Why limit ourselves to hearing only yesterday's records – do we want to end up in a time warp like the Rock 'n' Roll scene has? I certainly don't!

Remember, variety is the spice of life – let's be more open-minded about new releases, many of which would not be accepted by the funk crowd because they are by lesser known artists or on 'unfashionable' labels – let's give these new releases our support! At the same time, it is vital that DJs continue to make the effort to find and play top quality '60s records. I think that many of the best ever 'old-style' sounds have been unearthed in the last two and a half years, and my playlist at present is still seventy five per cent '60s. This is because I do not believe that the standard has deteriorated like certain other DJs do – they will find their popularity plummeting if they do not steer a course 'down the middle' – why not play the best of both! As a result, the quality of the music and the dance floor response will improve markedly. There's no doubt that if Wigan does close, the next successful all-nighter will be one that features predominately 'new sounds and exclusives with the oldies being an important but minor consideration. It's vital that we play the best possible selection available to us, instead of building barriers to stifle the brilliance of our music."

Whether or not certain sections of the scene chose to praise or slate him as a DJ, no one was ever in any doubt that Richard would stick rigidly to his principles when it came to his playlist: play the best, forget the rest. In the *Northern Noise* article, Richard referred to oldies as being 'an important but minor consideration', what then I wondered, were his thoughts on the success of the Oldies All-nighters at the Casino?

"I don't really have an opinion one way or the other. Undoubtedly they were hugely successful – I seem to remember that when Mike Walker told me they were to start, nobody really thought they would go that well! They did have an enormous short-term effect on the following night's event though; attendances went down to around 250–

Richard Searlings Current 'BIG 30' All-Niter Sounds

1 "Sad Girl" - Carol Anderson (Fee)
2 "I Don't Like To Lose" - Joe Matthews (Kool Kat)
3 "Where I'm Not Wanted" - Eddie Holman (Dynamo)
4 "He's So Fine" - Judy Street (Strider)
5 "I Won't Think Twice" - Eddie Jefferson (Goldwax)
6 "Is There Anything I Can Do" - Love Committee (Ariola)
7 "It Must Have Been A Broken Heart Attack" - Chester Pipkin (Omen)
8 "Can't Help Lovin' That Man" - Laura Greene (Grapevine)
9 "What Can I Do" - George Kirby (Cadet)
10 "My Baby Left Me" - Irma and the Larks (Fairmount)
11 "Wait 'Till I Get To Know You" - The Tomassos
12 "I Found True Love" - Billy Hambric (Grapevine)
13 "I Want My Baby" - Mel Britt (F.I.P.)
14 "I Wanna Do It With You Baby" - Performers (Mira)
15 "I Am Nothing" - Al Williams (La Beat)
16 "Showstopper" - Volcanos (Artic)
17 "Hold On" - Soul Generation (Notrayer)
18 "Born A Loser" - Don Ray (R.C.A.)
19 "The Price I Have To Pay" - Patti Young
20 "This Man In Love" - New Wanderers (Grapevine)
21 "Pretty As A Picture" - Little Richie (S.S.T.)
22 "Come And Go With Me" - Robert L. Martin (Didcot)
23 "The Lover Who Loves You Not" - Herbie Williams (G.W.P.)
24 "Something's Bad" - Nomads (Mo-Groove)
25 "Through Sleepless Nights" - Gene McDaniels (Liberty)
26 "Country Girl" - Christine Cooper (Parkway)
27 "Put That Woman Down" - John Leach (Lawn)
28 "Guess Who Loves You" - Frank Wilson (Soul)
29 "Just The Two of Us" - Del Capris (Sync 6)
30 "Turning My Sunshine Into Tears" - Len Jewell (Fontana)

SEARLING'S SAY SO!

The 'mod' phase, after looking at one stage like it could do severe harm to our scene, failed to make any impact whatsoever.

Quite simply, there are just too many good under-rated soul sides around at present for any self-respecting D.J. to even bother himself with ex-chart hits by SAM AND DAVE, BOOKER T. or PRINCE BUSTER!!!

Richard's playlist at the Casino in 1980, a regular feature in the Casino's Northern Noise. *As most of the titles are still under their cover-up names, how many can you identify, given that Richard himself could not remember some of them!*

300 – albeit a hard-core crowd who were definitely 'up' for the new discoveries. I used these sessions both as a testing ground for underplayed sides or new-found goodies, and for pyramid-building practice with the likes of Neil Allen, Dave Malloy and Keith Minshull!!"

I feel an explanation is called for. With all the surrounding controversy, 1979 was also the year that a group of Casino die-hards took it upon themselves to alleviate the bad vibes by building human pyramids on the dance floor. As Richard said, they began on one Saturday night following an oldies all-nighter, with the attendance well down and lots of room on the dance floor.

How or why a group of grown men decided to clamber onto each other's shoulders in order to build a three-tiered human structure is unclear, and will one day be the subject of historical study all of its own. What I do recall from those ridiculous incidents is that they always took place during Richard's spot, and if the construction team did by any chance manage to get the middle section in place, Mr Searling was always the one to attempt the leap from the stage onto the pyramid to form the top tier, whereupon the inevitable happened.

On a serious note, these 'testing ground' nights were the first place to come if you were only interested in the very latest sounds, and that meant not just '60s fans, but also those with an interest in the most up-to-date '70s soul from the US independent labels. Richard once said to me at the Casino: "What does the date on the record matter? The people who come here know what soul music is – it's the music that counts, not the decade!"

The first of the '70s tracks to feature in Richard's regular playlist in early 1979 included Larry Houston "Let's Spend Some Time Together", Roy Dawson's "Over The Top" (c/u James Mack & The Chicago Gangsters), Mike Jemison's "You'll Never Get My Love" (c/u The Men In The Moon) and the first two records to make me sit up and listen to modern soul, Bobby Thurston's "Just Ask Me" and Will Collins & Willpower's "Is There Anything I Can Do". Richard: "Quite simply, there were so many great and rare '70s indie tracks that John found for me, that I had to play them. There certainly wasn't a rebellion on the dance floor – in fact I even broke Eddie Holman's "This Will Be a Night To Remember" and Phyllis Hyman's "You Know How To Love Me" on the back of the '70s sounds like Larry Houston. To me, and to the Casino regulars it seems, it was the logical progression, the way forward."

As with Soul Sam, the desire to make the Northern Soul scene progress was Richard's main aim, but that progression did not mean that the scene had to lose its identity; between them, John Anderson and Richard managed to keep the old traditions of Wigan Casino alive by introducing the best quality records to the punters, and that quality was combined with rarity. As in the early days of the all-nighter scene, the people came to hear the sounds that they could not hear anywhere else – quality plus rarity equals rare soul.

"I think over its lifetime, the Casino brought Northern Soul into a much bigger arena, it filled the gap that was left by the Torch, Wheel,

Catacombs and other venues that were unable to remain open for one reason or another, becoming the anchor venue for what was a musical movement at the peak of its popularity. The commercialisation which came with the club was an inevitable by-product of its success and its appeal."

Could the scene have been better without the Casino's commercial ventures, as is the opinion of Soul Sam. Did they hamper its progress? "I don't think the Wigan Casino experience could have been any better than it was. When you look back at the records played there, they stand comparison to material played at any other venue, and to keep the quality so consistently high for eight years was an unbelievable achievement."

Over those eight years, Wigan Casino employed some of the scene's best DJs, but the quality of the music for which the club will always be remembered came from Richard Searling.

Finally, I asked Richard the impossible question: could he list his most memorable discoveries from the Casino? This list could have been much bigger and more comprehensive, but it still represents the absolute cream of what was a bumper crop of records first programmed by the Casino club from '73 to '81. Wisely, Richard stipulated that the list is not in any particular order of preference.

Richard gave the Casino and the Northern Soul scene a style and a class all of its own. A list of credits like this tells you just how important Richard was to the Casino and the scene.

- Vickie Baines "Country Girl" (Parkway)
- Al Williams "I Am Nothing" (La Beat/Palmer)
- Eddie Holman "Where I'm Not Wanted" (Acetate)
- Z. Z. & Co. "Getting Ready For The Get Down" (Columbus)
- The Group (featuring Cecil Washington) "I Don't Like To Lose" (Prophonics)
- John & The Weirdest "Can't Get Over These Memories"/ "No Time" (TIE)
- George Kirby "What Can I Do?" (Cadet)
- Tamala Lewis "You Won't Say Nothing" (Marton)
- Little Ann Bridgeforth "What Should I Do?" (Acetate)
- Jimmy Delphs "Dancing A Hole In The World" (Carla)
- Chris Bartley "I Go Out Of My Mind" (Acetate)

- The Combinations "Like A Good Girl Should" (Acetate)
- Billy Woods "Let Me Make You Happy" (Sussex)
- The Jades "I'm Where It's At" (Nite Life)
- Betty Boo "Say It Isn't So" (Acetate)
- Jackie Beavers "I Need My Baby" (Revilot)
- Ernestine Eady "Let's Talk It Over" (Phil La Of Soul)
- Eddie Daye & The Four Bars "Guess Who Loves You" (Shrine)
- Larry Houston "Let's Spend Some Time Together" (HFMP)
- Court Davis "Try To Think What You're Doing" (West Coast)
- Gene Toones "What More Do You Want" (Simco)
- Mr. Soul "What Happened To Yesterday" (Genuine)
- Lou Roberts "Everything You Always Wanted To Know About Love" (MGM)
- The Adventurers "Easy Baby" (Compass)
- The Volcanos "(It's Against) The Laws Of Love" (Arctic)
- The Delights "Lover" (Cuppy)
- The Appointments "I Saw You There" (Delite)
- Larry Clinton "She's Wanted" (Dynamo)
- Moses Dillard & The Dynamic Showmen "I'll Pay The Price" (Mack IV)
- The Lovers "Without A Doubt" (Frantic)

Part Three
THE BITTER END

"How could you begin to describe your feelings? Without the Casino, there was nothing. Nothing at all..."

Chapter Nine "TELL ME IT'S JUST A RUMOUR"

THE CASINO HAD many enemies. Some were blatant in their desire to see the club shut down, such as the police and a minority of the local population. Others, mainly out of self-interest, harmed the club by promoting their own ideas of how it and the Northern Soul scene in general should 'progress'. Levine and Curtis shed their links with traditional Northern Soul at the Blackpool Mecca in 1974, and ignited the '60s versus '70s debate, and there were invasions by numerous factions, from Mecca fans in plastic sandals to plastic Mods in fish-tail parkas, all of whom thought that they could replace our music with their own. All failed abysmally.

We did however, have one enemy with the power to end the all-nighters at any time – Wigan Borough Council. They owned the land on which the Casino stood, and despite the fact that Gerry Marshall owned the club and had a contract on the Station Road site, their plans to re-develop meant that they could enforce a compulsory purchase order and shut him down.

Rumours about the Casino's closure had been around since 1978, a major topic of conversation each week and another of the seemingly endless problems that the Casino had to overcome. By 1980, the whispers were getting louder. There were reports that Gerry Marshall had had talks with the Council about the club's future, and the outcome was not good. As 1980 progressed, the paranoia increased until every Saturday looked like it would be our last night. The Council made it known that they wanted to use the site for an extension of the Civic centre, and although no date had been set, this news was the first concrete evidence that, sooner or later, the 'Heart of Soul' would close.

Of course we all knew that it could not last forever, but when something becomes so important in your life, it's impossible to imagine life without it. Our fears were brought into focus though, in August of that year. It was a Saturday night when the bombshell landed.

Harpo, Wagsy and I arrived at the club around one o'clock as usual. The regular crowd were all there in our corner: the lads and girls from Stoke, Atlas, Geoff Oaks, Little Bob, Blondie, Karen and Christine Jones, and the North Wales crew, Dave Jones, Pip, Gabby and her sister Caroline.

Russ was at the decks as usual and the record bar was packed with regular collectors. Everything looked the same as ever, but we knew as soon as we came through the double doors that something was very wrong. There were looks of concern on peoples' faces that you just did not associate with a Casino nighter. The atmosphere was wrong; usually, the happiness of the Casino's crowd gave the place an air of excitement, even on the less well-attended nights, but the feeling that night was very different. Even so, when we heard the news it was so unexpected that it seemed impossible to believe. Atlas called me over and said: "Mike Walker is dead."

The Casino's manager, the man behind the whole concept of all-nighters at the club back in 1973 had died. This news was tragic

MIKE WALKER

Mike would have been in his element on the Seventh Anniversary Night. He would have been buzzing around the hall barking orders, checking everything was just right for the night of nights.

I still can't believe that he died last month. He, together with Gerry Marshall and myself were the instigators of the 'Heart of Soul' in September 1973. He did so much for the scene always full of ideas and highly talented enough to be able to carry them out. There will never be a replacement for Mike - the perfectionist and worrier - always time to talk things over and find out everyone else's point of view.

Mike loved the Northern Scene and the Scene loved him.

Maybe a few lines from his favourite record "Time Will Pass You By" - Tobi Legend could sum up how we feel.

"Life is just a precious minute,
Open up your arms and see it,
Give yourself a better chance
Because time will pass you right on by.
I'm just a pebble on a lonely beach
And I sit and wonder why . . ."

God bless you Mike.
RUSS WINSTANLEY.

Following the news of Mike Walker's death in August 1980, the anniversary edition of Northern Noise *carried this tribute by his long-time friend and fellow Casino original Russ Winstanley. Mike was irreplaceable. Everybody who knew him, will tell of his endless energy and total enthusiasm for our music. His vision in 1973 gave us the scene we have today, and soul fans owe his memory great respect. Mike's death really was the beginning of the end.*

enough, but the manner of his death hit us even harder. Mike had taken his own life. No one had the facts of what had happened in the right order, so the usual rumours spread quickly on the Casino grapevine. Even with this terrible news, the only thing on the minds of some people was the Casino's future: one rumour was that Mike had done what he did because of the club's imminent closure, and members of staff were pestered all night by people asking if this was true, and if so when and why. You can only guess the thoughts of Gerry Marshall and assistant manager Harry Green at our selfishness when they were mourning the loss of a friend and colleague.

Steve Whittle: "I had known Mike since 1972 when he first DJ'd at the Beachcomber, and later when he became resident DJ at the Palais de Dance (later Mr M's), so to me it was the loss of a great friend, not just an employer. I knew Mike was under pressure; he had invested a lot of money into RK Records in London, who owned Casino Classics. At first they did OK with the 'Three Before Eight' single, and the following release – "Loving On The Losing Side" by Tommy Hunt. Then they started to lose money – Mike in particular, when the following releases flopped. I was up at his house two weeks before it happened, and we stood in the garage where he actually died, talking about the Casino. Mike was always a worrier and a perfectionist, but strangely, that day he seemed fine, and if anything calmer than usual. I put it down to being away from the Casino and the pressures of work at the time."

Much to the relief of the regulars it was business as usual following the awful news. Preparations were in full swing for the 7th anniversary night in September, and they went ahead with Harry Green taking over as club manager.

The rumours of closure however, would not go away. Several meetings were held between the Borough Council and owner Gerry Marshall with the date for the site's re-development at the top of the agenda. When the anniversary night came around *Northern Noise* carried the following message:

"Since our last issue, a lot of things have happened, and unfortunately not many have been very good.

Russ Winstanley has taken over as editor due to the tragic death of Mike Walker last month – there's a tribute to him in this issue.

There is also the threat of closure clouding the celebrations of

Wigan Casino's 7th Anniversary. We hope to let you know one way or the other by the time we go to print."

At the anniversary, we were greeted by the news that the Council had put the Casino's demolition on hold for a while. There was a carnival atmosphere in the club that night. We were safe – at least, for a while.

But even in our celebrations, the more sober amongst us knew that this was the beginning of the end: soon, the Casino would be gone, and that was a fact we just had to be realistic about.

As 1981 dawned, the feeling of living on borrowed time began to abate. We had passed the 7th anniversary and made it to Christmas, and into the new year. These little targets were set and passed, and with each week that went by a sort of confidence returned. Not that it would really last forever, but we still had some time – perhaps another year – at our spiritual home.

February 1981 saw the 5th anniversary of the Oldies All-nighter. It was hard to believe that what had started out as an idea that the management thought would fail, had been going strong for five years. And going strong they were; the Saturday attendance had recovered from its slump in '79, and the attendance for the first Friday each month still regularly topped fifteen hundred. Perhaps the people who had been regulars in the early days and since left the scene, were coming back for a final fling, now that the club's demise looked certain. Where better to relive their memories than at an Oldies All-nighter, which played tried and tested favourites?

Gerry Marshall had been in regular touch with any changes of policy, and he was invited to attend a meeting at the Council offices. This time though, there was to be no good news. Re-development of the site would begin later in '81 or early '82. It was agreed that the Council should continue to lease the site to Mr Marshall until September, with a view to making the 8th anniversary the last night. This night would be September 19th, after which the Casino would be closed and demolished.

Gerry Marshall made plans to relinquish his ownership of the club after that last night. Those were the facts of the deal. Cold facts, however, can never tell the whole story: there were people who said that they were glad that the date had been set at last, to remove the uncertainty. Cheer up, they said, we still have a few months left, and anyway, we'll find somewhere else just as good as Wigan.

The 'End Of An Era' All-nighter was not only the best attended night that I can remember at the Casino, it was the most people that I have been under the same ceiling with!

Others said that they would be giving up the scene altogether after the last night, as nowhere would ever be as good as the Casino. Then there were people like me, who said nothing at all.

There was nothing left to say: Wigan Casino was to close, how could you find the right words to describe your feelings? Without the Casino, there was nothing. Nothing at all. I began to think of all the nights when, for some reason, girlfriends, finances, or whatever, I had not gone to a Saturday all-nighter, and I cursed myself for wasting the opportunity. Before the club had even closed, I was feeling deep regret for its passing. The Casino had been the focus of my attention for almost six years. School had gone, as had friends and girlfriends, but the Casino had always been there. How could I replace the biggest part of my life when it closed?

19th September, 1981. Exactly six years had passed since my first visit to the Casino, but they might as well have been six hundred: so much had happened during those years, so many great times, so much to look back on. It was just impossible to believe that it was about to end, that there would be no more visits to the 'Heart of Soul'.

In the weeks leading up to that night, there had been promises made to a hundred friends to keep in regular touch when the Casino closed. Friends who visited the club from far-off towns hundreds of miles from Wolverhampton, whom we had come to know better than our next-door neighbours. The North Wales crew, the lads from Sheffield and Barnsley, the girls from Northallerton, Burnley and Preston. The Gloucester lot, the Banbury crowd and the nutters from Scotland.

Never mind, we said, somewhere else would come along to be the next Casino, and we'll all meet up there instead. There was still the all-nighter at the Parr Hall in Rotherham, or the Fleet in Peterborough. But we didn't fool each other, any more than we fooled ourselves. The friendships that had been born in Wigan Casino would, to a large extent, die with its closure.

That night was memorable for several things: firstly, the truly amazing number of people who attended. On September 4th, the club staged a final Oldies All-nighter, and it was absolutely packed, even by the standard of regular Friday oldies nights, but the 'End Of An Era' night, as it was dubbed, was so full it was almost frightening. Both rooms, the balcony, record bar and every nook and cranny of the club were jammed solid with members, old and new.

But the biggest surprise was the news that this was not to be the last night. When producing the last night tickets to Mrs Woods at the door, we were each given a commemorative badge, a copy of *Northern Noise*, a poster and leaflet which read as follows:

"Welcome to the last Saturday Nighter…Due to the fantastic demand for tickets, and the fact that so many members have been unable to attend, we have managed to secure the Casino for just one more Oldies All-nighter on Friday, October 2nd…Tickets on sale at reception tonight, £3.00"

To me, this news made the 'End Of An Era' night a lot better than it would have been. Again, by some miracle, the Casino had managed to avoid the chop – albeit for a limited time – and the air of doom that had surrounded our journey up the M6 earlier that night was lifted. Others though, had a different perspective on the news. Many members saw the temporary reprieve as merely an exploitation of the club's popularity, a way of cashing in on our loyalty.

Steve Whittle: "I feel that the 'End Of An Era' night should have been it. Although the reason for the further nights after that did make sense, at least to Gerry Marshall. The lease agreement had a three-month notice period, which the Council chose to implement. Gerry would have been paying three months rent for the site even though the club was not open."

Again, business acumen took precedence over what the members of the club thought was the 'soulful' thing to do. Gerry Marshall was, first and foremost, a business man and a bloody good one. It should be remembered that without Mr Marshall's business brain, Wigan Casino would not have lasted for eight weeks, never mind eight years!

Steve Whittle: "To balance his books, it was decided to run another night on 2nd October, with the possibility of further nights until the end of the lease period. You have to remember, Gerry was not a soul fan. If the soul events had not been profitable, he would have replaced them with rock nights, punk nights or even whist drives to get people into the club. He had no pretensions about making the club into the 'Heart of Soul'. Wigan Casino was his business, it had been for twenty years – only eight of which had been reliant on the Northern Soul scene. To him, it was not cashing in, it was good business."

A lot of people decided, however, that September 19th would be their last all-nighter at the Casino. I remember running into Tony Warot in the record bar during the night, and asking him if he would be coming to the last night (meaning October 2nd). He replied: "As far as I'm concerned, this is the last night. Anything after tonight means nothing."

I shared in the feeling of being somehow let down, but part of me was just over the moon that it was not over – not just yet. I knew that this was not quite the 'End Of An Era', but when the end did finally come, I wished that September 19th really had been the last all-nighter.

MY TOP TEN FOR 1981

1	Nomads	"Something's Bad"	(Mo Groov)
2	Vivian Carol	"Oh Yeah, Yeah, Yeah"	(Merben)
		(c/u Roddie Joy – "Learning How To Dance")	
3	Charles Johnson	"Never Had A Love So Good"	(Alston)
4	Admirations	"You Left Me"	(Peaches)
5	Charles Brandy	"I Can't Get Enough Of You Baby"	(Blue Cat)
6	Ray Agee	"I'm Losing Again"	(Soul Town)
7	Vondells	"Hey Girl You've Changed"	(Airtown)
8	Richard Anthony	"No Good"	(Swan)
		(c/u Detroit Wheels – "Like A Good Girl Should")	
9	Jimmy Delphs	"Dancing A Hole In The World"	(Carla)
		(c/u Tony Hestor)	
10	Ike Strong	"Your Love Keeps Me Dancin"	(Noble)
		(c/u Lee Moore)	

Chapter Ten "DESTINATION UNKNOWN"

AFTER THE ANNIVERSARY night Harpo, Chris Plant and myself were DJing at a pub in Wolverhampton. We had done spots at the Cleveland Arms on and off for a couple of months and each Monday evening was spent there, planning the coming weekends' excursion. Except, that is, this night. There was no Casino to go to come Saturday as the 'last' Oldies nighter was set for October 2nd, a fortnight away.

I can remember deciding to do a Wigan oldies spot that night, as a sort of tribute to the club. Though the previous Saturday had turned out not to be the final event, everyone knew that this time there would be no miracle reprieve. I played some early Wigan stuff like the Sherrys' "Put Your Arms Around Me", J. J. Barnes' "Our Love Is In The Pocket", the Tomangoes "I Really Love You" and Williams & Watson's "Too Late". If anything, it made me feel even more fed up than before!

The imminent closure of the club was the only thing on our minds; it seemed to hang over everything else like a cold, wet blanket. It made the future seem uncertain, as though we were coming to the end of innocence. And the changes that were affecting our lives would be irreversible; the self-righteous teenager would soon be only a memory, along with the hundreds of friends that we would lose forever.

Change had always been an integral part of the scene. We had witnessed much over the years, but the biggest difference of all was the one which we ourselves could not see. The change to our own lives.

The lanky fourteen-year-old who had sneaked into the second anniversary back in 1975 bore no resemblance whatsoever to the pensive twenty-year-old of 1981. I had literally built my whole life around this decrepit and crumbling dance hall ninety-odd miles from my home, and in return, it had given me a sense of identity, and a pride in my lifestyle. And now it was all going to end.

On the 2nd of October, I was in a car with four others on our way to the Casino. We had just left the Old Vic in Wolverhampton, which had always been our meeting place for Wigan nights. The atmosphere in the car was the same as it always was on the way to the club; expectant, excited and slightly tense. We had all bought tickets for tonight before-hand, so we were assured of getting into the club, no matter how high the attendance. Nobody had even wondered out loud whether or not this was going to be the very last night.

We gave the appearance of a car-full of teenagers going to their favourite place, without a care in the world, just as we had done every week for several years before. Personally, I felt as though I were being driven to Crown Court to face trial.

I hated everything. I hated my workmates for their jibes about the Casino's closure, I hated my girlfriend for suggesting that: "Now that place is gone, perhaps you'll try to lead a normal life, like other people."

Fuck other people, and their 'normal lives'. Come to think of it, she could fuck off as well. The Casino had claimed yet another romance.

Now, sitting in this car driving to Wigan, my wrath was focused upon my fellow travellers, my mates. Why weren't they as gutted as me? Why were they still insisting upon talking bullshit about nothing of any importance? Was I the only sane person left in the world? The Casino, for Christ's sake, our Casino was closing down and all that these prats could talk about was "I wonder what time they'll open M's tonight?"

One member of our group, who had not been going to the club for very long, and was famed for the copious amounts of bullshit that he could fit into every sentence, began lecturing me on how good it was to get totally smashed out of his head on speed and dance all night. "I couldn't give a shit what record is playing" said this single-figure IQ. "They could play the theme from the fucking *Magic Roundabout* for all I care."

It occurred to me that this was all that was left for Wigan Casino. People like him, who jump on any bandwagon if they think it will improve their social standing. Who drive miles to the scene of an accident to revel in the glory of being able to say later: "I know what really happened, because I was there." Quite suddenly, I felt on the verge of tears. I leaned forward and said to Paul, the driver: "Paul, stop the car. Stop the car. STOP THE FUCKING CAR, MAN!"

He pulled over onto the side of the road and turned around to me with a bewildered look on his face. The rest of the group fell silent as well. I opened the door, got out and slammed it behind me. It was a five-mile walk back home, but I would have walked five hundred to get away from the Casino that night.

I didn't bother to ask what the night was like the next day, I already knew…"Thank you for your wonderful support for the last eight years…we've reached the end of an era…um, by the way, there's another last night coming soon…"

And so there was. I didn't know if I wanted to attend it, that is until I saw the date on which it would be held, and when I did, I knew I would be there. There was a perfect irony to it. Of all the days when they could have had the very last all-nighter at Wigan Casino, 6th December, 1981 was the most perfect, the most fitting.

The October event, so I'm told, was nowhere near as well-attended as the original 'last night', although over 1,200 people still felt the need to be there. Now the club would remain empty for two months until December 6th. Had everyone known about the three-month notice period on the lease agreement, they would have realised that that night would be the final curtain; the Council were not about to renew the lease when they had made plans to contract out the demolition of the club.

Unfortunately, the club members largely saw the December event as just the latest in a long line of rip offs. Sadly, Wigan Casino bowed out to a crowd of just over a thousand souls, and those who witnessed the funeral included some who had little respect for the deceased.

Friday, 6th December, 1981. The final chapter, the last all-nighter. As we drove along the M6 motorway to the Casino, the weather mirrored our mood – cold winds and driving rain. There was not much conversation in the car, and what there was, was short-lived.

This night I was travelling with a lad called Andy Wall from Kinver and his girlfriend Maria. I sat in the back of the car, remembering another rainy night on this road six years earlier, when Steve Slater and I had hitch-hiked our way to the second anniversary. Could it really have been only six years since my first visit to the Casino? It seemed as if that night had taken place in another lifetime, which in a way, it had. My life was so different back then, I was a schoolboy with no worries or thoughts beyond scrounging enough cash to get to the next all-nighter.

We stopped at the usual service station, Sandbach in Cheshire. Walking into the cafeteria, I passed the public telephone where Gamber and I had booked sixty-seven oldies anniversary tickets on that fantastic night in 1980; I remembered the two of us struggling to insert the coins in the slot because we were laughing so much, and the whole room being packed with soul fans in leather trench-coats, and all-nighter bags littering the floor…

There were perhaps a dozen people in the cafeteria that night, only one of whom was en route to the Casino. I walked over to Mark from

Gloucester and said hello. He had been staring out at the rain-soaked car park, sitting alone in a deserted corner. When he turned to me, a smile came over his face. He was as glad to see an old friend as I was, but that could not hide the tears that were welling up in his eyes. Mark was, and I hope still is, 'one of us'. He realised the importance of the night that was about to unfold as well as I did, and he felt the 'wind of change' that was in the air, too. I tried to be cheerful: "What do ya say, old lad?" But his face told me everything, there just weren't enough words to describe this feeling of dread at what was coming.

An hour later we had left the motorway. We turned left at the island at the end of the exit road and took the A49 into Wigan. The houses along the way were dark and lifeless, the wet rooftops shining yellow under the neon street lamps. Houses full of people who led normal lives, from school to work, from work to the pub, meet a nice young lady, settle down, have kids and slog for the rest of their lives trying to pay the mortgage. And occasionally, go back down to the pub and forget about the blandness of their existence. The words of my ex-girlfriend came back to me: "Now that Wigan is gone..."

Wigan was like my home town. It was full of young men just like me; standing at the crossroads between youth and adulthood, unsure about the future and suspicious of the present. You didn't have to look hard to find those 'normal people'. These were the lads who used to pick fights with the soul crowd who walked up Station Hill to the Casino from the trains. A good night out for them was sinking fifteen pints, staggering to the fish and chip shop and starting a ruck on the bus home.

If they were really lucky that night, they might capture the drunken attentions of a female of the species; equally plastered, and dressed for the evening's 'sponsored pub crawl' or hen party in an eye-catching little off-the-bum number. Together, these people used music in the same way that they used toilet paper. There was nothing more profound about them than the depth of their pint-pots or Bacardi and cokes. I loathed them.

We finally pulled onto the car park across the road from the club and I saw that neon sign shining for the last time: 'Casi Club'. There was no rugby scrum at the main doors, just an orderly queue, waiting to get in out of the rain. They could have been waiting for a bus.

Mrs Woods was still on the door, just as she had always been. The door-men were still dressed in their evening clothes, just as they had always been. But the air of expectation had gone, and replaced by a feeling of resignation. Conversations were whispered and hushed, faces no longer beamed, gazes were directed towards the floor. The lads from hundreds of towns who had once greeted each other like long-lost brothers could no longer find the words. It was terrible.

I walked up the stairs and into the small corridor. The manager's office was still there, but of course Mike Walker was no longer hurrying people along, and fretting over some minor detail that would make the night run much more smoothly. Mike was gone forever, along with the good times.

Entering the main room, I realised that something else was missing. There was still a wave of heat that you always felt as you came in, though not as intense as in earlier days, but that smell, the rich aroma of sweat, talcum powder, cigarette smoke and deodorant that had always greeted me, had gone. It had been replaced by a musty, mouldy stench of mildew and dry-rot from the walls and the floors. The place had stood empty for two months and it smelt like death.

There had been no cleaners in the place since the last nighter in October, and the tables and radiators were still covered with two-month old coke bottles, the carpets still littered with paper and coffee cups. So this was how the most famous disco in the world was to bow out – a dirty, smelly shadow of its former self. The Casino had never been the 'poshest' venue in the world: any regular will tell you horror stories of the state of the toilets, or how the carpets were full of cigarette burns and old chewing-gum. Gerry Marshall had never wanted to spend any time or money on refurbishments, knowing that the Council could revoke the lease agreement at any time. Besides, any attempt to change the Casino's appearance would have been met by a storm of protest by the members, who liked things just as they were. But this night the building looked as though the demolition work had already started. Our club was dying before our very eyes.

Although the night had been billed as an oldies all-nighter, the musical policy was almost irrelevant. Russ and the DJs played a mixture of classic Casino tracks alongside some of their regular Saturday records. Mr M's opened at 3am as usual, and the night was, outwardly anyway, just like a normal Saturday. Needless to say though, it was anything but a normal Casino atmosphere.

Two years earlier, I had witnessed a Wigan crowd turning nasty. It had been on the night that Russ had played a reggae record. As this night wore on you could sense a feeling of unrest amongst the people on the dance floor. It was nothing tangible, nothing that you could point a finger at, but there was still this underlying edge; people had begun to gather in conversation, as though secrets were being passed around. Towards the end of the night, each record was applauded more and more intensely, and shouts and whistles started echoing around the club. Nothing individually significant, but the combined effect created an unsettling atmosphere, everyone was tense, although, no one would have been able to explain why.

Most of the night was spent saying goodbye to old friends. I think that was the saddest part of all; despite the promises of meeting up elsewhere in the future, we all knew that this time, goodbye meant goodbye forever. I remember seeing Caroline from Kidderminster standing on the edge of the dance floor in our corner, arms folded and head down, tears running down her cheeks. What could you say to make it easier?

Wandering around the club that night brought memories flooding back of the club's earlier days. The record bar where I had bought and sold prized items from my collection. I recalled my best ever deal: the Inspirations' "Your Wish Is My Command", Theo-Coff Invasion's "Lucky Day", Donna Coleman's "Your Love's Too Strong" and Don Varner's "Masquerade", all for £15 from Neil Allan from Stoke. On the balcony, I remembered my first visit in '75. I had stood in the same spot that night at about 5.30am, watching the first rays of light stream over a dance floor that was packed solid with anniversary revellers, feeling the thrill of being part of it for the first time, feeling a part of me would always belong to this wonderful place...

At just after 7am, Steve Whittle began winding up his final spot in Mr M's, which as ever, had been full all night, and the dance floor gave rapturous applause and cheering after his final record: "The Night" by Frankie Valli & The Four Seasons. Steve has been offered £400 for the record since the Casino closed, simply because it was the last ever record in Mr M's. He told me recently that he wouldn't sell it for £400,000.

As M's closed, a great flow of people came into the main room for the final hour. Russ had taken over at the decks, and fittingly, he would be the last DJ just as he had been the first back in 1973.

Although the club had not sought an extension to the normal closing time of 8am, it soon became clear that it would not close on time. The dance floor was packed, there were very few people sitting or standing at the edges; it seemed that everyone in the club felt the need to be out on the floor for one last time.

They shouted in unison: "SOUL!! SOUL!!" They stamped their feet so hard that I felt the floor would give way under the strain. A mood of hysteria was taking over the Casino, a realisation that we were present at the passing of a legend, and for some, the moment was too much.

People had started to take souvenirs as mementos; the ashtrays had long since disappeared, so anything removeable was taken. Even today, it's hard to believe what some people wanted to take home with them. They smashed tables and chairs so that they could claim a piece. They took the valves off the radiators. They tried to steal the EXIT sign above the main double doors. They pulled pieces of plaster from the walls, and they even tried to break the mirrors on the supporting beams.

I watched in horror. Was it not bad enough that this was the end? Why did they have to make it worse by acting like a bunch of idiots? This was not what Wigan Casino was supposed to be all about. Casino people had always been the coolest of the cool, the best of the best. The rest could go to their plush nightclubs and drink themselves into oblivion, or fight themselves into hospital, but soul people would always be the best. What I was seeing had nothing at all to do with the music and the people with whom I had grown up. Their hysterics and their almost violent displays of emotion sickened me.

At about 8.30am, after the last three records had been played for the third time, I stood on the edge of the floor, as a girl who could not have been more than fifteen-years-of-age, pushed her way off the dance floor. Her face was streaked with tears and mascara, and in her hand she held a small piece of wood. As she brushed past me, I realised that her trophy for the evening was part of the dance floor. She had dug up a piece of floor that had been danced on for eight years by countless soulies.

Others were not slow to catch on; after all, what better souvenir could there possibly be of Wigan Casino than the actual dance floor? Knives and other implements appeared and their owners got down on all fours and began digging up the most sacred part of the club.

Andy and Maria had already left the club, and they told me they would wait in the car for me. At about 8.40am, Russ played Dutch Robinson's "Can't Get Along Without You", and I danced. I was bumped and barged from all sides by the other dancers who crammed the floor. Years ago, if two dancers had collided accidentally, both would shake hands and apologise, and probably go on to become firm friends. That was the Wigan way, the reason for the wonderful atmosphere, and the mutual affection that was such a part of the scene. Tonight, all I got from the other dancers was a scowl, and the occasional "fuck off!".

As the record finished, I found myself for the first time ever, actually wanting to get out of the club before the night had finished. I had to go. The 'Heart of Soul' was dead, and this was just bullshit pretending to be the real thing. I didn't stop, I walked off the floor, through the double doors and down the stairs.

As I walked out into the cold and bleak morning, I didn't look back at the club. It was Saturday, December 7th, 1981. That day was my 'coming of age', the end of adolescence and the start of adulthood – the last ever all-nighter at Wigan Casino had taken place on my twenty-first birthday.

I got into the car where Andy and Maria were chatting. As I got into the back, Maria passed me an envelope and leaned back to plant a kiss on my cheek. "Happy birthday, Dave" she said. As I looked at the birthday card I just said: "Yeah. Can we go home now?" I had seen a lot of tears that night, but when mine came I thought they would never stop.

At 9.10am, Russ played the very last record: Frank Wilson's "Do I Love You (Indeed I Do)". By that time, we were already back on the M6 for the journey home. Somewhere along the way, I swore to myself that I would never set foot in the town of Wigan again.

In March 1982, fire swept through the empty building, destroying the front offices, the stage and the dance floor. In February 1983, the Casino Club was demolished. Some time after the demolition, Wigan Borough Council let it be known that they had made a 'financial mis-calculation' in their plans to build an extension to the town's Civic centre on the site, and the centre would not now be built. They apologised to those connected to the former club for any inconvenience caused by their oversight, and stated that the club need not have been demolished after all.

The site of the club was eventually redeveloped. First a supermarket was built, and later a job centre. Since the demolition of both of those buildings, the Station Road site remains empty.

Chapter Eleven "THIRTY SPECIAL RECORDS"

ACCORDING TO STEVE Whittle, the only way to compile a list of your favourite records is to write out the first one hundred, then screw them up and start again on the ones that you missed. Our music is so diverse that you need a top one hundred for each category. This list covers most of them, and each track holds a very personal memory.

30. EDDIE PARKER "Love You Baby" (Ashford 1)
(E. Lewis, J. Coleman, Jack Ashford) Detroit, 1968

My good friend Dave Evison used to play this record in most of his oldies spots at the Casino, and he would introduce it by saying: "And now for the Northern scene's National Anthem..."

I don't want to make sweeping statements for every record in this list, but if you could bottle the essence of pure Northern Soul, you would hear this track when you pulled out the cork. There have been many uptempo records played over the years; some possessed a frantic beat and a heartfelt vocal track, others though less soulful, were great dance records. Only a handful of these tracks had everything – manic beat, brilliant instrumental breaks, soulful female backing, and a lead vocal that would raise hairs on a snooker ball. Of those that did, "Love You Baby" is one of the best.

Written in 1968 by Detroit soul man Jack Ashford for his own label, this storming slab of soul features the backing vocals of The Ebonies, one of whom was Mrs Jack Ashford, better known to the soul world as Lorraine Chandler. The beat never lets up from the first bar, and if possible, it seems to get faster. Eddie Parker needs no introduction to soul fans. His screaming, searing voice leaves its indelible impression on you not just with this track, but also his other just as perfect Northern classic, "I'm Gone" (Awake).

When you remember that most rare soul tracks were cut in a one-room studio, without the modern technology available to today's performers, you begin to realise the incredible talent that created Black America's soul sound in the '60s, a talent which, with the obvious exceptions went largely unheard and unrewarded. To cut a track as perfect as this, with all the arrangement and instrumentation involved, is not down to luck. It is genius.

29. THE VALENTINOS "Sweeter Than The Day Before" (Chess 1977) *(Mary Wells, Cecil Womack)* Chicago, 1966

Chess Records, incorporating its sister labels Checker and Cadet, form one of the biggest catalogues of blues, R&B and soul music in America, stretching back to the late forties when the industrial heartland of the country began to establish its own identity through music. As in the other great centres of Black American music – Detroit, New York and Philadelphia – Chicago soul was heavily influenced by gospel and inspirational music, and this track is a perfect example of how the black youth of the time took their musical heritage and turned it into a secular and individual reflection of their lives and experiences.

"Sweeter" is an energy-packed, vibrant expression of pure joy, from the immaculate production to the tight, vocal harmonies of the Womack brothers. All the ingredients are there for a perfect Northern Soul record; just add one jam-packed Oldies All-nighter at the Casino, garnish with one square yard of dance floor (if you could find one!) and light the blue touch paper. Sweet Lord, what memories.

28. RICHIE ADAMS "I Can't Escape From You" (Congress 238) *(Jerry Ragavoy, Richie Adams)* New York, 1966

The intro to a record – that very important first 30 seconds – is the deciding factor for a dancer determining whether or not he/she is going to stay on the floor, drift back to his/her mates for a chat, or fight for a space in which to do his/her stuff.

When the intro to this record played to a Casino crowd, it rarely failed to fill the floor to over-flowing. The brilliant piano riff which leads into the thumping drum beat just gets under your skin, and I would defy anyone with an ounce of soul in their veins to sit still when it's played.

That haunting, ominous piano returns later during the song as it builds to its climax, and Richie belts out the vocals in great style, telling the world how he just can't do without his woman.

This is the kind of record that reminds you of why you chose Northern Soul above any other music.

Sheer perfection.

27. RAY POLLARD "It's A Sad Thing" (United Artists 50012)
(L. Reed, G. Stevens) **New York, 1966**

It's hard to imagine a more different record to Richie Adams than this, but in its way it has all of the same appeal, and more. The beat never rises above mid-tempo, but you danced to "Sad Thing" for reasons other than developing blisters on your feet.

This record is quite simply a purists' dream; a sorrowful, painful story of what it's like to lose your love, packed with so much soul that you are carried along and immersed in its emotion. The orchestral backing takes you to wonderful peaks until the final, crushing conclusion – she's gone, and she's never coming back...

Dear reader, if you have never heard this record before, move as many mountains as necessary to listen to it. And please explain to me why a man who can bring tears to your eyes with the searing power of his voice slipped into obscurity, whilst the pampered brats of the pop world grew rich from their media-hyped drivel?

I have never owned a copy of this record, and I don't ever want to. I would hate to take something this good for granted, it's better just to hear it now and then at an all-nighter or soul night, or on tape in the car, so that I'll never lose the thrill of that wonderful voice.

Most all-nighters had and still have a regular 'last record'. Wigan had "I'm On My Way". Stafford had "It's All Over". Gary Kellet, an old friend from Preston once said to me: "This record is good enough to play at the end of the world." I couldn't put it better than that.

26. SAM WARD "Sister Lee" (Groove City 205)
(Sam Ward) **Detroit, 1966**

Yet another Detroit record with that churning backbeat which was the rare soul trademark in the early '70s. Right from the sharp drum intro and the ever-present guitar work, this is a record which was just made for all-nighters. The female backing is more than a match for Sam's wailing, powerful vocals, typical of the excitement that Black America generated in such abundance during the '60s.

Dancers and collectors alike will know "Sister Lee" so well, that it's daft to try to analyse it too deeply. Just ask the DJ for it at your next all-nighter or soul night and hit that floor!

25. DEON JACKSON "I Can't Go On" (Carla 45-1900)
(Deon Jackson) **Detroit, 1965**

Picture the scene: April '83 at Stafford's Top Of The World's first anniversary all-nighter. Later on we would witness a scintillating performance by Harold Melvin and the Bluenotes, but now, Harpo and I are in the record bar, scanning the sale boxes for long sought-after US imports. I've got about £35 to spend, and it's burning a hole in my pocket because I can't decide whether to blow the lot on a copy of Lee Bates' "Why Don't You Write" or wait and see if anything else turns up.

Harpo suddenly pulls a 45 out of a pile and thrusts it under my nose. It's a white Carla demo of Deon Jackson. "There you are mate! I told you I'd seen one somewhere!" I take it out of its sleeve and study the run-out groove to see if it has the original matrix stamp, which would indicate whether this copy is an original Detroit release or one of the later second issues from New York. Unlike Harpo's copy, which he had played earlier that night at his flat as we prepared for the all-nighter, it is not a Detroit original.

"How much is the Deon Jackson, mate?" I ask the seller. "Err…giz a tenner" replies the lad sitting behind the sale box.

I turn to Harpo again. "What d'you reckon, Harp?" He shrugs and chews his lip. "Put it this way, are you going to find a better record for sale in here tonight?"

Lee Bates will have to wait until the next nighter. Buying this record was as memorable and as exciting to me as Harold Melvin's live show. Deon Jackson, unlike many of his contemporaries did enjoy a measure of commercial success in his native land. Many of his Detroit Carla recordings were nationally released on the Atlantic label, giving his great musical talent the kind of exposure that it deserved, and several sides were also released through Atlantic's UK outlets.

A wonderful, soulful vocal performance.

24. CONNIE CLARK "My Sugar Baby" (Joker 716)
(Frank Wilson) **Los Angeles, 1966**

My most treasured and vivid memories of September 1975 and first visit to Wigan Casino include this brilliant record. The piano and drum intro still make the hairs on my neck stand up, even twenty-three years after I first heard it.

Written and produced by soul legend Frank Wilson, whose other credits include the classic "Do I Love You (Indeed I Do)" for Motown's Soul label, this uptempo belter has been played on the oldies circuit ever since its Wigan debut in 1973, and I'm sure it features in the top ten of many followers of Northern Soul over the years.

Coincidentally, there is a male vocal version of the record which is supposedly an unreleased acetate of the author's original version, and it's dynamite! But although it sounds like, and probably is, Frank Wilson, to me it just doesn't compare to Connie's frantic classic.

23. THE SILHOUETTES "Not Me Baby" (Goodway 101)
(Earl T. Beal, Richard A. Lewis, Cornelius Brown, John Wilson)
Philadelphia, 1968

Once again I'm indebted to my old mate Harpo for introducing me to this gem. Copies of the original are very scarce indeed, because it was never intended for release as a single. The 45s were only produced to plug the band's tenth anniversary album, and were attached to the album cover.

The record itself is as perfect an example as you can get, of the tight group harmonies that became the trade mark of Philadelphia soul. The power of the lead vocal contrasts superbly with the lighter tones of the rest of the band, which still retain a hint of the 1950's 'Doo-Wop' style for which the Silhouettes were first recognised.

A mid-tempo beat with brilliant brass breaks make this a perfect and very memorable dance item, but for me, the record's strongest attribute is the lyrics. When delivered by such a fantastic voice they become so powerful that you find yourself singing along with it on the dance floor. You believe this guy when he tells his woman it's over, that he's been taken for a fool for the last time…"If some guy should make you cry, who'll do your thinking, who's gonna dry your eyes? Not me baby…" That's the way mate! Show her who's boss!

22. DANNY WOODS "You Had Me Fooled" (Correc-Tone 1052)
(B. Williams) **Detroit, 1965**

Back to the Motor City once again for this masterpiece. There is so much going on in this record that you feel differently about it with each successive play. On a dance floor you only get the raw emotion that comes from a 100% pure R&B classic. It commands you to dance, and you obey. But when you listen again in the comfort of the car or at home, you get the full effect of the clever and unusual arrangement from Detroit soul stalwart Sonny Sanders, and how it compliments Danny's pleading vocals. It has all the basics of a blues ballad with the tinkling piano intro and constant guitar licks, but the whole thing is so much greater than its individual parts. You can label it R&B, blues, deep soul or whatever, but you have to concede that the one category that really sums it up is 18 carat Northern Soul. Danny later found fame on both sides of the Atlantic with Chairmen Of The Board, but I don't think he ever made a more perfect side. They just didn't come any better than this.

21. REPERATA & THE DELRONS "Panic" (Mala 758)
(Green, Marchand) **New York, 1968**

Has there ever been a record more perfectly suited to the demands of the dance floor than this monster? With material like this, Russ and Co. set the standard for the rest to follow. The beat never lets up from the manic intro to the frantic finale, complimented by the sugar-sweet vocals and that crazy whiplash drum effect.

But there's a lot more to "Panic" than just a perfect beat. Listen to the lyrics, if you grew up with the record like me, you must have sung them a hundred times on different dance floors, and you realise that this girl is in urgent need of a cold shower to calm her hormonal activity! There is certainly nothing of a gospel nature in the inspiration behind this song, you can't get more worldly than a tune written about sexual frustration, can you?

The group did have chart success in the UK with "The Captain Of Your Ship" although that flopped in the States, and "Panic" had some national airplay when it was re-released on the Casino Classics label. This, whatever your thoughts on the rest of C. C.'s output, was a real Wigan monster, and despite the fact that constant plays over the years have made it rather too familiar for a scene that has been spoiled by so many great discoveries, it still stands as one of the all-time best Northern Soul stormers.

20. ARTHUR PRYSOCK "Hurt So Bad" (Old Town 106)
(R. Hart, Tony Randazzo, R. Wilding) **New York, 1974**

Originally performed by Little Anthony & The Imperials in 1967, this slab of deep soul is just about as far removed from the mainstream

Northern Soul sound that you can get. I don't think it was ever played at any major venue either, and its inclusion here is purely one of self-indulgence. Why? Because it is by far the most anguished and soulful record that I have ever owned, and with luck, some enterprising DJ will give it a spin and realise that this is potentially a massive all-nighter sound.

Arthur's vocal talent is reminiscent of the best of Gene McDaniels; deep, rich and so expressive that you just have to sit up and listen. The female group harmonies are there too, as well as a beat that gathers pace as the record reaches its crashing climax.

But all of those ingredients only give the record dance floor potential, the real joy of the song is in the lyrics, or rather the pain, which tell of the hurt of seeing a long-lost love in the arms of another: "I know you don't know what I'm going through, standing here looking at you..."

God I love it! Everyone should hear it and make it the monster that it should always have been. As the old saying goes: "Soul as deep as you like...and then some".

19. JIMMY CONWELL "Too Much" (Gemini 1003)
(Leonard Smith, Jimmy Conwell, Godoy Colbert, Ralph Graham)
Los Angeles, 1967

The more astute reader will have noticed that I have a great fondness for the lyrics of a song as much as its dance floor appeal. This comes from a high regard for the writing talents of the people who worked on the small independent labels in the mid-sixties in America, from where most of the music that we adopted as our own originated. High on the list of those unsung heroes is the late west coast writer, arranger and producer Leonard 'Jewell' Smith.

Len Jewell, as he was better known to fans of his multitude of Northern Soul classics, not only co-wrote "Too Much" but also recorded another much-loved dancer with the same backing track entitled "Bettin' On Love" for Fontana. As dance records, it's hard to say which is the better of the two, but if you are a lyric junkie, there is no contest, because "Too Much" has quite simply the most gritty, angry and heart-felt lyrics of any record you are ever likely to hear.

You can almost picture the scene. 3am in a down-town LA bar, and Jimmy is staring into his Jack Daniels as the bar tender says: "Jimmy, wha's wrong wit' choo maan?" Jimmy looks up with blood-shot eyes and replies: "What started out to be such a good thing, has taken my pride and replaced it with shame. I can't face my friends 'cause I know what they're thinking, now I understand why some men start drinking. I'm like a drowning man in a sea of misery, never thought this could happen to me. I'm smoking more but enjoying it less, I get a whole lot of sleep but I don't get enough rest. I'm wound up in sorrow, like thread on a spool, it's no good feeling to know you've been somebody's fool. It's a no good feeling at all, it's too much, just too much for one heart to take..."

Oh Lord, to be able to write like that. Just once, just once...

18. THE DEL-TOURS "Sweet And Lovely" (Starville 1206) *(McDaniels, Ways)* Chicago, 1969

Another of Richard's plays from late '79 and early '80, and one of the prime examples of the Casino's ability to unearth previously unknown '60s tracks that would have graced any venue in any era.

Storming Chicago soul epitomised; frantic drum rolls, clever guitar work and breathless saxophone breaks, along with several neat changes in direction half way through to keep the more acrobatic dancers happy. The uptempo beat is complimented by some excellent group harmonies from start to finish – in fact there's so much in "Sweet And Lovely" that you wonder if they threw the bath tub in for good measure!

Very much one for the '60s purists, and the record gained massive popularity on the dance floor as well as a cult following with the collectors in the record bar. I remember Walsall DJ Chris Plant getting a copy of it in 1980, probably from John Anderson at Soul Bowl, and instantly becoming the envy of the dealers and collectors.

17. WILL COLLINS & WILLPOWER "Anything I Can Do" (Bareback BBR 531) *(J. Wright, Tom Bridwell, R. Weekes)* New York, 1977

I first heard this at Wolverhampton's Lafayette club when Soul Sam was guest DJ one Monday evening. Harpo does a mean impression of Sam introducing it by the cover-up title: "This is the Love Committee and "Just Call My Name"...

Being a '60s only fan in those days, the record went over my head and stayed there for months afterward, but when I realised that Northern Soul did not have to always be fast and on a label pre-dating 1st January 1970, this was one of the first modern tracks that I really fell in love with.

Personally, records like this strike a chord in the memory of my love for the sweet soul of the Stylistics, the Delfonics and the Detroit Spinners in the early '70s, before I had even heard of Northern Soul. "Is There Anything I Can Do" is every bit as much a love ballad as the Delfonics' "La La Means I Love You", the difference between them is that the Will Collins track is also a brilliant dance record. To dismiss material like this as just disco, which I admit to doing myself, is short-sighted to say the very least!

Collins' voice is just as expressive as that of the Stylistics' Russell Thompkins Jnr, the Detroit Spinners' Phillip Wynn or the Delfonics' Major Harris, and the production values match those of famed producers like Van McCoy and Thom Bell; tight group harmonies, clever rhythms, catchy hooklines, and of course, the powerful, heart-felt lyrics: "I just want to make you see, how much you mean to me...You are the sunshine of my life, that's why I want you to always follow me...Just call my name, and I'll be right there."

OK, so we had our favourites, and we argued our corners a little too much sometimes, but as Richard Searling said: "How can anyone with an appreciation of soul music fail to see the quality in stuff this good?"

16. BOBBY THURSTON "Just Ask Me" (from album "Sweetest Piece Of The Pie" Mainline 12747) *(Willie Lester, Rodney Brown)* Merriville, VA, 1978

Another modern track in the same vein as Will Collins is this brilliant Casino shuffler, also played in '79. Of all the modern soul that Richard spun, I think I would have to put this at the top of the heap. Drawing another comparison to the Detroit Spinners, this has very much the same feel as "Just Can't Get You Out Of My Mind".

Like Danny Woods' "You Had Me Fooled", Thurston's cut appeals to the armchair soulie as well as the dance floor animal; a lot of the record's content is just not audible to you in an echoing dance hall, it deserves a one-to-one on the stereo or the car's cassette deck.

While researching for this book, I played the track at home – the first time I had heard it since the Casino closed – and I was amazed at just how good it is. It has a quality that sets it apart from any particular decade, or any particular era for that matter. There's no doubt that it is, and always will be, associated with the Casino, but even that accolade puts too many restrictions into the mind of someone who has never heard it.

It's just soul, pure and simple. Listening to this again made me wonder why on earth we had to put our music into such restrictive categories in the first place.

15. BENNY MAHAN "She Knows How"
(Scratch/Pompeii 45-66690) *(W. Carson)* New York, 1966

This record totally blew me away the first time I heard it, and it still does now, fourteen years later. Originally played at Stafford, it has never been played by any DJ for any length of time, and what a criminal waste of a brilliant rare soul gem that is!

I bought my first copy in 1984 from a lad from Cannock for £10, and back then it was considered to be just a 'living-room favourite'. Rare, collectable, and much admired, but not thought to be good enough to become big. Or, in my opinion, just too good for the average dance floor.

The record features a very 'laid back' production, with a fabulous guitar hook-line that sticks in the memory after a few plays. As it builds, "She Knows How" has so many clever rhythm changes and vocal high-spots that you need a few spins to take it all in. Benny's pleading voice tells the world how his woman really turns him on, and finally the orchestral climax which builds throughout the song is enough to "Chill your bones", as my mate Wagsy used to say.

My first white demo copy was sold to ex-Wigan DJ Gary Rushbrooke at an all-nighter at Stafford's Top Of The World in 1985. Like me, he fell in love with it on the first time of hearing it, and he just had to have it. Which he did for £25 cash and the same amount in swaps!

I bought a yellow issue copy for £30 some time later, then sold it for £50, financial considerations being foremost in the deal.

I've since managed to find another copy of what still remains one of my favourite 'feel good' records.

14. THE VOLCANOS "(It's Against) The Laws Of Love"
(Arctic 115), *(C. Fisher)* Philadelphia, 1966

How do you describe a record this good without going over the same old cliches? If you know it, then the chances are that you regard it as just another oldie from the early Casino days; good in its day, but a bit played out now. But that ignores the true appeal of the record, and again I found the best way to re-discover material like this is to hear it away from a club, in the calm of the living room. There is so much to love about it, that you feel you are hearing it for the first time; those subtle chord changes and haunting rhythms compliment the vocal harmonies and the perfect mid-tempo beat so well, but the true story behind the record is once again to be found in the lyrics: "You've been staying out late, not saying where you've been going. Don't wanna believe you love someone else, but I'm gettin' tired of foolin' myself, and it's against the laws of love, what you've been doing."

This record is another perfect example of how to combine a serious love song with a killer dance beat. A treat for the ears as well as the feet.

13. THE INSPIRATIONS "No One Else Can Take Your Place" (Breakthrough 8152) *(L. Ivey, L. Bell, H. Bell, J. Gibson)* Hollywood, 1977

This is going to surprise a few people. The song was first recorded in 1967 and played on the scene some ten years later. Neil Rushton wanted to issue the track in the UK on his Inferno label, but discovered from label owner, Joey Jefferson, that the master tape had been lost. The re-recorded version features the lead vocal of Charles Diamond, and although the backing is identical to the original recording, his brilliant, expressive performance just gives the '77 item a slight edge.

12. BOBBY HUTTON "Come See What's Left Of Me" (Philips 40601) *(Jo Armstead, Bobby Hutton)* Detroit, 1968

I am grateful to Gaz Kellet from Preston for giving me a tape of this record in 1984, when it was first played at Stafford's Top Of The World and covered up as Casanova Bennett.

This heart-wrenching floater was penned by Hutton and Chicago legend Joshie Jo Armstead. Bobby had another big Northern Soul success with the Blackpool Mecca and early Wigan record "Lend A Hand", taken from his 1973 album "A Piece Of The Action", but this Giant Production is so different. "Come See" is a mournful, achingly soulful mid-tempo item, a prime example of what became known in the '80s as the beat ballad.

The date of the record is hard to judge, which also makes it a good crossover candidate; it has elements of mid-sixties Detroit with the Jo Armstead influence but Bobby's vocal is so complex and powerful that it might have come from early '70s Philadelphia. But again, why bother to dissect it?

I dedicate the inclusion of this record to everyone who thinks that soul music has nothing to do with the Northern Soul dance scene. "Come See" is the proof that the people who unearth rare soul for our scene still have their priorities in the right order – soulful content always comes first. Absolute perfection.

11. EDDIE DAYE & THE FOUR BARS "Guess Who Loves You" (Shrine SR-112) *(Harry Bass, Carl Kidd)* Washington DC, 1966

Now we're getting serious. From one of the most collectable labels ever, comes two minutes of pure Wigan Casino, circa 1979. Without any doubt, this is one of the best and most sought after records that the Anderson and Searling connection ever gave to the Northern scene.

Formerly covered up as Frank Wilson, Richard had this at the top of his playlist for almost two years, even amongst the other material that was surfacing in the last months of the Casino. A class dance record, and a prime example of the main room fare that helped sustain an interest in newies when the all-nighter took over as the main attraction at the club.

Everything is there for the ideal Northern Soul side; the crashing drums, the time changes and the soulful voices – the only thing that detracts from the record is the lyrics. Not that they are crass or hackneyed, it's just that, even after listening to the record countless times over the years, I can't understand any of them! But that does not spoil the overall atmospheric feel of the track, if anything it adds to it.

Still one of the super rare records on the scene even today, I don't think there are more than three or four copies of the original in existence, and they would sell for nothing less than a four figure sum these days.

A record that evokes memories is common, but a record that brings back crystal-clear flashbacks to your favourite place in your favourite time is a very rare thing. "Guess Who Loves You" does just that.

10. BIG MAYBELLE "Quittin' Time"/"I Can't Wait Any Longer" (Rojac 115) *(Jack Taylor)* New York, 1968

Do yourself a favour. If you are reading this with no experience of soul, and believe that Pink Floyd made meaningful records or that Phil Collins is a great singer, get a copy of this or any of Maybelle's recordings. Perhaps her deep soul ballad "Do Not Pass Me By", and learn the error of your ways.

This double-header is the epitome of '60s soul; the real music of Black America that went unheard and ignored by a world spoon-fed on the trite and bland.

Maybelle's life was one of pure tragedy. A life wasted on drugs and booze, and a career ruined by scheming record producers. And yet when she sang, it was with a force and a joy that still stands today as a reminder of her sublime talent. Take the soulful voice of Esther Phillips and the gospel inspiration of Mahalia Jackson, stir them together, and you have an idea of Maybelle's vocal ability.

But there was something more to that voice; an edge, an anger that came perhaps from her life situation, giving her music a gritty tone and the listener an uncomfortable feeling that this lady knew what it was to feel pain.

On this release, she gives both sides of her moody vocal range. "Quittin' Time" is a storming up-tempo dancer, full of drum rolls and rhythm changes just right for the dance floor, with the band almost struggling to keep pace with Maybelle's slick and powerful voice.

"I Can't Wait Any Longer" is another dance gem. Mid-tempo, and the slower pace gives her more room to express her emotional message with that begging soulful voice: "I just can't wait any longer, my love is getting so much stronger. I need your lovin' so bad… It seems my lonely days are getting longer, and it's driving me mad…"

In life, Maybelle cut a sad and pathetic figure, ravaged by self-abuse and cheated of her true worth. In death, her legacy, through records like this, will live as long as people still marvel at the wonderful heights that were reached by the creators of soul music.

9. DAMON FOX "Packin' Up" *(Damon Fox, Thom Bell)* (Fairmount FA-1021) Philadelphia, 1965

This record is the most exciting one minute forty-six seconds ever put onto vinyl. It's hard to give it any marks for style or sophistication, but for raw, gritty in-your-face soul dance music, it is unequalled.

Right from the simple piano intro and first crashing drum roll, you know what to expect. The production values are not particularly high, and there is certainly nothing much to be heard in the way of an arrangement, but that in no way detracts from the record's appeal. If anything, the lack of sophistication adds to its overall feel. This is the genuine article, simply a bunch of guys in a small studio in 1965.

How they put their raw talents together is how our music came about; with energy and enthusiasm, ad–libbing and making their own rules as they went along.

Soul Sam gave the track to the scene in 1978, when he played it at various all–nighter venues – The Palais, Nottingham, St. Ives Leisure Centre and Leeds Central – covered up as Don Parker. It was this record, along with William Powell's "Heartache Souvenirs", that formed part of a swap deal with Richard Searling, in which Sam obtained two big '70s tracks, Z. Z. & Co's "Gettin' Ready For The Get Down" and Larry Houston's "Let's Spend Some Time Together", as part of his switch from '60s soul to modern in 1979.

By pure coincidence, I was flicking through a 1976 copy of the collectors' fanzine *Soul Cargo* some time later, which featured a full label listing for Fairmount Records. And sure enough, there was Damon Fox's "Boney Maroney" with "Packin' Up" credited as the flip side. In other words, one of the biggest dance tracks ever played on the scene, a record that was successfully covered up for almost a year, was known about and actually listed two years earlier.

For me, this record will always bring back sweet memories of being on that Casino floor on a newies night, surrounded by friends: Harpo, Wagsy, Atlas, Geoff, the twins Paul and Noel, Gabby…knowing when to try another spin or to clap in unison with the other dancers, trying to keep up with the frantic beat for a minute and a half, and applauding the DJ when it ended. Absolute heaven.

8. DANNY MONDAY "Baby, Without You" (Modern 1025)
(*J. Ford, L. Vegas*) Los Angeles, 1966

Back in 1975, the biggest dance floor sounds at the Casino were Kenny Smith's "Lord, What's Happening To Your People", The Idle Few's "People, That's Why", The Tomangoes' "I Really Love You", Joe Hicks' "Don't It Make You Feel Funky" and Skullsnaps' "I'm Your Pimp". When any of them were played, the dance floor would be full. In fact, just the intros to those top sounds were enough to send a thrill through the dancers.

But one of my abiding memories of those early days was the crowd's reaction to this record. They would knock over chairs and kick bags out of the way to get to the floor when they heard the stunning intro to this classic. The word that comes to mind when describing "Baby, Without

You" is power – absolute unbridled power. That driving backbeat raises the hairs on your neck, especially when played at full volume, as it always was at Wigan. The female backing is perfect, as is the horn section which repeats throughout the track, but Danny's pleading vocal stays with you long after you think that you've had enough of it, or that it's just another oldie. There can't be a dance floor that has not at some time been full of soulies singing along with the first verse's immortal opening lines: "Somebody call me a doctor, somebody call me a nurse. Do something for me, don't let me suffer. Please! don't let it get worse!"

Pep was the first DJ to treat us to the record back at the Catacombs, but this monster will always be associated with the Casino's first years, which, like "Baby, Without You" were so full of energy, and so full of power.

7. HERBERT HUNTER "I Was Born To Love You" (Spar 9009) *(Malcolm Gayden)* Nashville, 1967

When looking for the perfect example of just what I believe is Northern Soul, this track, along with Gloria Jones' "Come Go With Me", is the one that I quote. Anyone who spent any time on the scene, particularly at the Casino, would have been very familiar with the record, so its hard to preach to the converted about just how good it is. But to those who don't know it, "I Was Born To Love You" has just about everything; magical intro, driving beat, unusual changes between the verse and chorus to give the dancers plenty of scope to do their stuff, and above all (yes, you guessed it) a voice and lyrics that will tear your heart out.

Written by Malcolm Gayden, who was responsible for many of Robert Knight's hits in the '60s and early '70s, such as "Branded", "Everlasting Love" and "Love On A Mountain Top" this record appeals to just about everyone; collectors because of the rarity of original copies, dancers because of its great uptempo beat, and even those who didn't dance or collect loved it for those heart-breaking lyrics.

"I really miss you baby, if something should spoil your plans, just turn around and there I'll be standing here awaiting, anticipating that you'll come back…"

It really does come out of the top drawer as far as our music is concerned. Herbie's classic stands the test of time, still sounding as fresh and strong as when Soul Sam first played it at Cleethorpes all-nighter back in 1977.

6. JACKEY BEAVERS "I Need My Baby" *(Don Davis)*
(Revilot 208) Detroit, 1966

Collectors of rare soul tend to have favourite record labels, and will avidly buy up everything on that label they can find. Others go a step further and buy up everything that they can find on a label specific to a particular city. And out of all the cities in the USA, the most bountiful, most revered and most collected has got to be Detroit.

Although the home of Motown, to the rare soul collector the true Motor City sound came from the multitude of small, independent labels that surfaced during the sixties: Golden World, Ric-Tic, Groovesville, Magic City, D-Town, and in the case of this special record, Revilot.

The label was well-known and much respected in collecting circles during the Casino years, and issued many discs that later became in-demand Northern Soul 45s – the Parliaments' classic "Don't Be Sore At Me", Rose Battiste's unbelievable "Hit And Run" and both versions of the dance floor favourite "Our Love (Is In The Pocket)" by J. J. Barnes and Darrell Banks spring to mind. It had something for most collectors; an impeccable pedigree, boasting the production talents of Don Davis, Dale Warren, Mike Terry and George Clinton, amongst others. And this track is the jewel in the crown.

"I Need My Baby" is as close to being the perfect rare or Northern Soul record as it could be. To hear it played at the Casino in 1979 was unforgettable. It typified Richard's playlist, oozing soul and emotion, with that stirring, mid–tempo beat. This was a record that went so much deeper than the trite and pop-orientated stompers being played by other DJs at the time.

Added to which, although the record comes from a well-known label, copies of it were – and still are – to quote Atlas from Stoke: "as rare as rocking-horse shit". A record with everything; soulful, impossible to find, and above all, that magical something that makes it sound as good today as it did at the Casino in '79. And, as it did in Detroit in 1966.

5. CHARLES JOHNSON "Never Had A Love So Good"
(Alston ALSX-3571) *(H. Straws, Nathaniel Dean)* Miami, 1979

This is one of those rare, as in few and far between, records for which you just do not need a category, because to limit its appeal by aiming it at a single group of listeners or dancers would be an absolute sin.

Listen to this record and you can see why Soul Sam raved over it, and why everybody on the scene, fell in love with it. Even a die-hard '60s fan like myself in '79 had to admit that records as good as this stood comparison to anything else being played at the time: it stands on its own even amongst the modern soul of today, such is its timeless quality.

Of all the modern releases that have been introduced to the Northern scene since Wigan, this is my absolute favourite. Right from the opening bars it just floats along on an endless wave, and Charles takes you on an emotional ride as he tells you about his love. It's magic. Pure soul perfection.

I remember Alan Rhodes playing Millie Jackson's "House For Sale" at the Casino, and introducing it with the words: "I always thought that this record was too soulful for Wigan." Too soulful for the 'Heart of Soul'? I didn't understand what he meant then, but hearing this track for the first time back in '79, reminded me of Alan's words, and I can see now what he meant. Records like this are so good that they should never be taken for granted or forgotten like just another oldie.

"Never Had A Love So Good" is a perfect reminder of why you got into soul in the first place, and a prime example of what the rest are missing out on.

4. MR SOUL "What Happened To Yesterday" (Genuine 150)
(B. Hall, M. Soul)

Unless they are amongst the more serious collectors, people who loved this record at Wigan, will probably not recognise it from its true title and artist credit. Back in '79, Richard had this covered up as Maurice McAllister "Your Love Is Slipping Away", and that is how it was known for over ten years until other copies surfaced.

This really is a DJ's dream discovery. The label and artist are truly obscure, making it far easier to prolong the record's 'shelf life' as a top sound – which indeed it proved!

Of the song itself, what can you say? With a deep, rich vocal similar to the likes of Roy Hamilton, Gene McDaniels or Arthur Prysock, and a stunning brass arrangement over a moody mid-tempo beat, this record is close to the top of the pile as far as Casino classics are concerned.

I bought an acetate of the record at Stafford all-nighter in '84 for £20, still unaware of the true identity of the artist. Curiously, a copy was found with the same label number, but the artist was credited as Al

Scott. Presently, there are no more than a handful of copies in circulation, each with a value of around £1,500.

The owner of one of them is our old friend Soul Sam. I remember one night at the Stewpony Arms soul night when Sam was at the decks, he called me over and said, "Wait until you hear what's on next!" and he covered the record with his hands until it started playing. As you might imagine, having once owned the record and still not knowing who really sang it, it was a lovely moment. I rushed onto the stage to get a look at the label for the first time ever.

The only problem was that whereas I used to have the record, albeit only in acetate form, and not knowing the artist, I now knew the artist, label and no longer had the record, because I sold it about ten years ago. Sometimes, collecting rare soul really pisses you off.

3. GLORIA JONES "Come Go With Me" (Uptown 732)
(C. E. Quick) New York, 1966

The ancient Egyptians were buried with objects that they believed would help them in the afterlife. I have decided that my copy of this truly wonderful record is going in the box with me when I go, so that I can organise a rare soul scene in the hereafter.

This record should be in the collection of everyone who purports to have any appreciation of Northern Soul; quite simply, it is the best female vocal of all time, and that is one sweeping statement to stand by.

Gloria was the wife of the late Marc Bolan, and her life was touched by personal tragedy in the well-documented car crash which claimed his life and very nearly hers too. That may be how the world remembers Gloria Jones, but to anyone connected to the scene, she will always be the 'First Lady' of Northern Soul through her sixties recordings such as "Tainted Love" and this slab of pure perfection from the influential New York label Uptown.

The whole production and arrangement of the record give it an atmospheric feel which is amplified in the steamy heat of an all-nighter: the mono recording techniques of the '60s have the ability to 'echo' through a sound system in the way that today's complex stereophonic, digitalised, computerised and sanitised methods never could.

The staple ingredients are there: brisk 4/4 beat, the female chorus, and Gloria's untouchable, soulful voice. But the most memorable thing is the vibrophone that repeats its simple two chord pattern from start to finish, echoing hypnotically over the beat and the vocals like the icing on the perfect cake.

Again, it is impossible to give a true impression of just how brilliant this record is by just writing about it. If you know and love it as I have for the last twenty odd years, it needs no introduction. If you've never been fortunate enough to hear it, the only way to fully appreciate it is to hear it played in the rarified atmosphere of a packed all-nighter. Well? What are you waiting for?

2. BOBBY TAYLOR & THE VANCOUVERS "There Are Roses Somewhere In This World" (Sunflower 126) New York, 1972

Without wishing to blow my own trumpet, I think it's fair to say that after twenty-five years of going to soul events and buying and selling rare soul records, I've seen an awful lot of the Northern Soul scene. Consequently, the venues which I still attend on a regular basis hold few surprises. These days the things that I look forward to are those special moments which happen every now and then; running into a long-forgotten friend, seeing a long-coveted record in a sale box, or in this case, hearing a record for the first time in years.

That moment came at the 'Togetherness' all-nighter at Stoke's King's Hall on 4th July 1996. Pep was doing the final hour of what had been a brilliant night, and two of his final three records were Ray Pollard's "It's A Sad Thing" and Bobby Taylor's "There Are Roses". Dancing to them again was just magical.

Canadian soul man Bobby once recorded for Motown's VIP label, where he cut the superb "Oh, I've Been Blessed", but this track outshines even that gem. His powerful voice is complimented perfectly by the Vancouvers, and the great guitar work blends with the uptempo beat in a tight, seamless arrangement perfect for the dance floor.

Great dancer though it is, I have positioned this record as high as number two for one reason – yes, you've guessed it – the lyrics. There are probably five hundred other tracks that I had to leave off this list, many of which are equal to "Roses" in dancefloor terms. However, Bobby's classic has a strong message in its lyrics – it's never too late, you have always got hope. OK, so your love-life has turned to shit. Most do at some time or other, but there is always that dream: "And you can bet we will make it girl, because there are roses somewhere in this world for you and me."

Don't look for lyrics of such inspirational quality in anything other than a soul record, because they just don't exist; in all of the examples that I have included in my top 30, the lyrics perform just as important a rôle as the dance beat.

If all that you require from music is 'a nice tune' or something to listen to whilst driving, my elitist and self-righteous advice is: stick to pop music. But on the other hand, if you require something deeper and more meaningful, something that reflects true life and offers solutions to its problems, and a music that will stay in your veins forever, then look no further.

To complete my list of all-time favourites was the most difficult aspect of compiling it, but logically, I had to pick a Wigan classic.

1. "THE GROUP" (featuring Cecil Washington)
"I Don't Like To Lose" (Prophonics 2029) *(Billy Tuthill)*
Mount Morris, Michigan, 1966

As this record has already featured in a previous chapter, and because there has been so much already written about its history, the best thing to do here is to review its content. Easier said than done.

It has everything that makes up a Northern Soul classic: powerful vocal, girlie backing, the perfect beat, rhythm changes and spine-tingling instrumental breaks. So do a thousand other records that I had to omit from this list. What makes this so special?

Perhaps the minor key guitar intro, or the "I don't like it, I don't like it" from the backing vocals, or even Cecil Washington's vocals themselves, so threatening and ominous: "All the people laugh they say, I'm a foolish one. But see who laughs last, when I begin the fun..."

The answer is all of the above, in conjunction with the 'X' factor – that unknown ingredient which makes "I Don't Like To Lose" the record which, more than any of the countless sounds that were played at the club, transports me back to the main room of the Casino in 1979. If "Love You Baby" is the essence of pure Northern Soul, then this record is the very bricks and mortar of Wigan Casino.

The Reverend Cecil Washington was an unlikely figure to become a soul celebrity, or even to have made another record after this one – and just who 'The Group' were has long been forgotten.

Equally mysterious is just why a man of the cloth should feel the need to sing such non-spiritual lyrics as: "You see, I don't like to lose, and there's nothing about it in the rules. And no matter what happens to me, I'll always be on top – you'll see!"

The true identity of the artists is, of course, totally irrelevant. The record was covered-up for so long that, in the minds of those who raved over it, the track will always be attributed to Joe Matthews.

The climax to the record is perhaps its most dramatic part, as the horn section goes into overdrive, along with the backing girls. The final verse tells the whole story of the song: "And I'm gonna do it. I'm gonna make it. So people, start moving – get out of my way! Or I'll walk right over you, and I'll do it today! 'Cause I'm gonna make it – I'm gonna win! WIN!!!!" The track ends with a final guitar lick, which runs into an eerie vibrophone trailing into the dark…

And there you have it, the record that is – in my elite opinion – the best ever made. First played by the best DJ of the best club on the planet.

Chapter Twelve "TIME MARCHES ON"

IT HAS BEEN almost twenty-six years since the Casino's first all-nighter, and an equally unbelievable nineteen years since its last. After the closure of the club, the Northern Soul scene went back to its roots; a small, underground movement found in isolated pockets around the country. Wigan's demise left a massive void in the scene. There was no longer a central venue for devotees to patronise, and of those venues that continued to run soul events, none was ever as regular or as phenomenal as the Casino. Starved of a regular, well attended all-nighter at which to break new sounds, the rare soul scene began to die out. And the inevitable happened – the Northern circuit became an oldies only scene.

Not that this was due to any lack of opportunity. In 1982, a monthly all-nighter began at the Hinckley Leisure Centre under promoters Chris King and Terry Samson, at which there were many excellent live performances from the likes of Major Lance, Edwin Starr, Junior Walker, Curtis Mayfield and Chuck Jackson. There were also occasional nighters at Notts Palais and all-dayers at the Birmingham Locarno and Stafford. But there was nowhere with the format to continue to bring new sounds to the scene, and very few DJs who even tried. That was until two veterans of the '70s soul scene combined to give rare soul a new lease of life. Dave Thorley, an ex-Yate DJ, and Keith Minshull started a twice-monthly all-nighter at a superb Mecca venue, the Top Of The World in Stafford.

Under the banner of the Top Dog Soul Club, the club combined the best of the north and south in its DJ line up: Richard Searling, Pat Brady, Gary Rushbrooke, Dave Withers, Adey Pountain and Yate's top man Ian Clark. Together with Soul Sam and the '60s Soul Mafia', otherwise known as Guy Hennigan and Keb Darge, they gave rare soul a new dimension in the early to mid-eighties. Stafford was never going to be another Wigan, but it had a loyal and knowledgeable crowd who could appreciate the high quality of the records that were played there. For a few years, Stafford was the place to be for lovers of the music that the Casino had been famous for; with its top DJ line up playing the best new sounds to the best crowd, it earned the accolade of being a 'mini' version of the Casino. Included amongst the records first played at Stafford were:

- Chuck Holiday "I Still Love You" (Gloria)
- Soul Brothers Inc. "Pyramid" (Golden Eye)
- Jackie Day "My Naughty Boy" (Phlectron)
- Lee Bates "Why Don't You Write" (Instant)
- Bobby Sheen "Something New To Do" (Warner Bros)
- Larry Davis "I've Been Hurt So Many Times" (Kent)
- Johnny Gilliam "Room Full Of Tears" (Cancer)
- Kell Osbourne "Law Against A Heartbreaker" (Highland)
- The Empires "You're On Top Girl" (Candi)
- The Brilliant Korners "Three Lonely Guys" (Modern)
- Sam Dees "Lonely For You Baby" (SSS International)
- Johnnie Honeycutt "I'm Coming Over" (Triode)
- Sam Fletcher "I'd Think It Over" (Tollie)
- Danny Moore "Somebody New" (Alrite)
- Big Frank & The Essences "She Won't See Me Cry" (Blue Rock)
- Norma Jenkins & The Dolls "Aeroplane Song" (Maltese)
- The Brooks Brothers "Lookin' For A Woman" (Tay)
- Eric Mercury "Lonely Girl" (Sac)
- Bobby Hutton "Come See What's Left Of Me" (Philips)
- Bud Harper "Wherever You Were" (Peacock)

Proof, if it were needed, that rare soul did not die with Wigan Casino, as many predicted it would. Stafford was an excellent venue, which came along at just the right time. There were some very memorable nights, especially the live acts such as Harold Melvin & The Bluenotes, Chuck Jackson, Eddie Holman and a fantastic Detroit Revue, which included Lorraine Chandler and Eddie "Love You Baby" Parker.

The club itself was well-known to the Midlands soul crew, as there had been a regular all-dayer during the late '70s. The Stafford venue ran alternate Sunday events with the famous Locarno Ballroom All-dayer in Birmingham, and whichever club was open became the final destination for our weekend after the Saturday all-nighter at Wigan.

The Top Of The World was an interesting and refreshing venue. After the closure of the Casino, things got stale very quickly on the Northern Soul scene, with only oldies venues doing anything like regular business. Stafford came along at exactly the right time for disillusioned soul fans, whose adult attitude and knowledgeable enthusiasm was one of the biggest reasons for the success of the club.

It was always interesting for us, or rather, those of us who enjoyed a cynical swipe at 'normal' nightclubbers, to see the perfumed hoards who attended the 8pm-2am session. The soul crowd were admitted at midnight, but then ushered upstairs into the smaller room until the end of the 'normal' night, whereupon both rooms were taken over by the all-nighter. To my eternal shame, I have to admit that, together with Dougie from Stafford, we would occasionally infiltrate the alien environment of the white stiletto shoes and the tattooed knuckles, in order to re-affirm my long-held belief that normal discos were total shit.

```
DEDICATED TO ALL THE KNOCKERS WHO RECKON THERE ARE NO 60'S STYLE OBSCURITIES
LEFT, WE PROUDLY PRESNT THE 'MIDNIGHT EXPRESS' TOP 50 FOR '83/84............
 1. SHE WON'T SEE ME CRY - BIG JOE'S IVORY BRASS(C/U)
 2. COME AND SEE WHAT'S LEFT OF ME - BOBBY HUTTON(PHILIPS) "CASANOVA-BENNETT C/U"*
 3. MOVE IT BABY - SINGING SAM WARD(DAN-DY)
 4. CHAINS OF LOVE - KENNY GAMBLE(ARCTIC)
 5. IT'S A HEARTACHE - LITTLE CHARLES(DECCA) "SAM COLTRAINE C/U"
 6. WALK ON INTO MY HEART - BOBBY SMITH(AMERICAN ARTS)*
 7. CAN'T DENY THE HURT - THE PROPHETS(VERVE) "COURT DAVIS C/U"
 8. SWEET SWEET KISSES/IT'S OKAY WITH ME - LARRY WRIGHT(A GO GO)
 9. MAKE YOUR MIND UP - JACK MONTGOMERY(C/U)
10. SO SAD - THE RAMBLERS(TRUMPET) "UNITED FOUR C/U"
11. MY LOVE GETS STRONGER - TOMMY RIDGELEY(INTERNATIONAL CITY)
12. GONNA TAKE A CHANCE - THE CHANDLERS(C/U)
13. WE COULD BE SO HAPPY - THE PREMONITIONS(JADE)
14. YOU GOT ME LOCKED UP - AARON VARNELL(C/U)
15. WOULD I DO IT OVER - THE ULTIMATIONS(MAR-V-LUS) "NORMAN JOHNSON C/U"
16. HOOK, LINE AND SINKER - ROY WRIGHT(MICA) "BOBBY LEE"/"BOBBY TREETOP C/U"
17. WHEN YOU'RE ALONE - GEORGE JEFFERSON (C/U)
18. TREASURE THAT CAN'T BE FOUND - BUD HARPER(C/U)
19. GO FOR YOURSELF - THE ANTIQUES(LA SALLE) "FRANK WILSON C/U"
20. I WALK ALONE - CLIFFORD BINNS(C/U)
21. I AIN'T GOING NOWHERE - MELVIN DAIVS(C/U)
22. THAT'S JUST WHAT YOU DID - LARRY LASTER(DUO VIRGO)
23. PROUD GUY - MONROE TAYLOR(CHESAPEAKE)
24. HEARTBREAKERS LAW - JIMMY GRESHAM(C/U)
25. I'VE GOT TO KNOW HER NAME - JOHNNY HAMPTON(C/U)
26. LOOKING FOR A WOMAN - BROOKS BROTHERS(TAY) "AGENTS C/U"* *
27. I'M STILL YOURS - JOHNNY SUMMERS(YORKTOWN)
28. WITH ME YOU'LL WANT TO STAY - PHIL ORSI(C/U)
29. BABY BE MINE - THE VENTURAS(DANIELS)
30. THERE'S SOMETHING ABOUT YOU THAT SENDS ME - IMAGINARY VISIONS(C/U)
31. LONELY MAN - THE UNIQUES(LENNAN)
32. YOU GOT IT - BILL BRANDON(MOONSONG)
33. IF IT AIN'T ONE THING - THE SPIDELLS(CORAL)
34. GOT TO BE A LOSER - THE ARCADES(TRIAD)
35. MY BABY - EDDIE BANKS(ROBERE)
36. LEAN SOUL DADDY - LITTLE ANN(RIC TIC ACETATE)
37. I'LL BE HAPPY - THE JADES(NITE LIFE)
38. THE AEROPLANE SONG - NORMA JENKINS(MALTESE)*
39. YOU FOUND SOMEONE NEW - LEON WASHINGTON & PARIS(C/U)
40. SWEET AND KIND - GORDON KEITH(C/U)
41. WHISPER YOU LOVE ME BOY/STEP BY STEP - CINDY GIBSON(ARCTIC)
42. ANY GIRL IN LOVE - IRENE & THE SCOTTS(C/U)
43. WHAT'S YOUR NAME, WHAT'S YOUR GAME - EXPERIENCED HEARTMENDERS(C/U)
44. CARFARE BACK - HERB JOHNSON(ARCTIC)
45. I WAS WRONG - THE NEW YORKERS(C/U)
46. YOUR LOVE HAS GOT ME - AL WILLIAMS & THE MASQUERADERS(C/U)
47. I JUST CAN'T GET ENOUGH OF YOU BABY - CHARLES BRANDY(BLUE CAT)
48. NOT LIKE YOU BOY - BARBARA CHRISTIAN(BROWNIE)
49. LONELY GIRL - ERIC MERCURY(SAC)
50. SHE'S GOT GOOD LOVING - TERRIBLE TOM(C/U)
```

During the heyday of the Top Of The World All-nighter in Stafford, the excellent fanzine Midnight Express *produced this answer to those who claimed that the rare soul scene had died with Wigan Casino!*

Dougie, being of similar opinion, loved to watch the procession of drunken girls and boys as they performed their weekly rituals; the girls crying hysterically for no apparent reason and the boys punching the hell out of each other because somebody had bumped into them at the bar. Great fun.

When the last of the dross had finally been forcibly ejected from the club, ('Leave it Wayne, he's not worth it mate!!') the main room echoed to some top class soul from the best line-up of DJ talent in the country.

There was a good atmosphere of 'musical tolerance' on the dance floor, with '60s, '70s and '80s records given equal appreciation: you could hear a '60s stormer like Larry Davis' "I've Been Hurt So Many Times" followed by a sophisticated '80s soul 'floater' like Booker Newbury III's "Love Town", which was played when it was a Top 10 hit. The mood of the regulars just seemed to be, never mind the decade, if it's got soul, play it. Richard Searling's doctrine at Wigan Casino had finally caught on!

Even the upstairs room which served as the obligatory oldies room did things a little differently. It soon gained a reputation for playing only the more unusual type of oldie, the type only to be seen in the record bar, and normally only heard in the front rooms of the more knowledgeable collectors. A small cross-section of the oldies room menu shows how different and enjoyable Stafford was to the discerning soul fan:

- Ernest Mosely "Stubborn Heart" (La Cindy)
- The Sweethearts "Beauty Is Just Skin Deep" (Kent)
- Jock Mitchell "Not A Chance In A Million" (Impact)
- Edwin Starr "You're My Mellow" (Ric-Tic)
- Nolan Chance "If He Makes You" (Constellation)
- Don Varner "Masquerade" (South Camp)
- Eddie Parker "I'm Gone" (Awake)
- Margie Joseph "One More Chance" (Volt)
- Moses Dillard "I'll Pay The Price" (Mack IV)
- Matt Lucas "You Better Go-Go" (Karen)

The oldies DJs (Chris Plant, Pete Widdison, Nick Marshall, Dave Greet and Dave Alcock) showed the way forward for all other oldies venues, although sadly, few realised the potential of their ideas. Eventually, the Top Of The World All-nighter became a classic statistic for the local constabulary. When the club passed out of the Mecca chain and into private ownership, the law brought pressure to revoke the all-night license, claiming that local crime statistics went up on all-nighter Saturdays. There was such a desire by the police to stop the soul functions, that pressure was applied to oppose the club's drinks licence. Inevitably, Stafford went under, but not until it had single-handedly rescued the rare soul scene from the depression of the Casino's demise. Thank you Dave Thorley, it was great.

There was also Warrington, which ran on alternate weeks to Stafford, Blackburn, Leyton Buzzard and Whitchurch in Shropshire, which I will always remember because it was the first all-nighter that I ever DJ'ed at.

As the nineties approached, the scene continued to attract new faces and promoters ran all-nighters and soul nights up and down the country. In the '90s, a new format took off – the 'Weekender'. Seaside towns with large holiday camps of the Butlins' variety playing host to up to five thousand soul fans three or four times a year, and the popularity of the events at Yarmouth, Southport, Cleethorpes and Fleetwood grows greater each year.

As we enter the new millennium, Northern Soul is on the crest of a huge wave of popularity again, due in part to the release of many compilations of '60s and '70s records on CD for the first time. But this time around, it cannot be labelled as just 'Northern': the movement has taken root in all parts of the UK, with a large and growing contingent of fans in the capital. But even amongst the people who have joined the scene in the nineties, there is still an almost religious fascination with Wigan Casino. And for the people who attended the Casino, it still remains the 'Heart of Soul'. Conversations with friends from that era still centre on those sweaty nights that we spent dancing the night away. Time has changed our lives, but not our memories.

What of those friends today? Harpo has two children, Beth and Jonathon, and still attends soul venues. Steve Slater is divorced and can be found in most wine bars and clubs in Wolverhampton, usually chatting-up a young lady. Wally and Caroline from Kidderminster eventually married and now have a family. Cleo from Worcester got married and plays saxophone in a night club band. Most of the Wolverhampton crowd married, started a family and eventually returned to the scene.

And Wagsy? He quit his job in a Dudley health club a few years ago, went to live in Wigan. He still has more teeth than a comb, and is still one of the best friends I have ever had.

And what of the DJs today? Richard Searling is one of the biggest crowd-pullers on the scene, and as well as working most of the top all-nighters, he now hosts the popular soul show on Manchester's Jazz FM.

Pep lives and works in Wolverhampton at his town centre record shop. He is one of the busiest event organisers on the scene, running several regular soul nights in the area, as well as the occasional all-nighter.

Soul Sam is one of the most respected and revered figures on our scene and like Richard, still keeps the faith after almost thirty-five years at the top Northern Soul venues. His enthusiasm is still an inspiration to the rest of the scene.

Russ Winstanley still DJ's and had a busy time promoting the 25th Anniversary of the Casino. It was the first time I had set foot in Wigan since that last fateful all-nighter in 1981, and my return put a full-stop to work on the book.

Steve Whittle is one of the country's top oldies jocks, and does the rounds of all-nighters and soul nights. As I mentioned earlier, he was Best Man for my first wedding back in 1985. After the ceremony, the two of us went to watch Wolves play Wigan Athletic at Molineux, and after the evening reception, my wife and I went to Stafford's Top Of The World All-nighter with Steve and his wife Kim. Well, can you remember your wedding night with the same clarity as me? I think not!

Of the other Wigan DJ's, Dave Evison, Pat Brady, Ginger Taylor and the evergreen Keith Minshull are still all-nighter regulars. Gary Rushbrooke quit the scene in 1986 and 'Mr Oldies', Brian Rae, continues to confound the laws of nature by managing to attend more venues than most. God bless the lot of them!

And me? I'm not married anymore, but five years ago we had our first child, Mitchel. The name was my idea: unknown to the wife – until now that is – it's a tribute to the singers whose surname is

Mitchell, namely Stanley ("Get It Baby"), Phillip ("Free For All"), Dave ("The Trip"), and Jock ("Not A Chance In A Million"). He has already shown a healthy interest for my record collection, and despite one or two lapses of musical appreciation, (Spice Girls etc.) I am confident that I can steer him in the right direction, to ensure that he is a soul boy of the future!

Sadly, a few people have never returned to the scene, and I have lost all contact with them: Danny from Sheffield, a great mate and a fellow collecting maniac, Dave Jones from North Wales, the man who once walked from Knutsford services on the M6 all the way to Wigan, and the girl with the scene's sexiest bum, Gabby from Bangor. Wherever you all are, I hope that you are happy and that life is treating you well, I'll never forget you.

It has been a labour of love to write this book. Every chapter holds many happy memories, and to work in collusion with old friends and much-admired personalities from the Casino to write those chapters has fulfilled a life-long ambition. But I wish that I did not have to complete the picture by writing about the friends that did not make it.

As a teenager, the most important thing in the world should be your own happiness, and how you achieve it becomes, in later years, your mental scrap book: the events that you look back on and say wistfully: "Those were the days…" To a teenager, death is something that happens to elderly relatives or to people with little or no bearing on their own lives. Bereavement is easier to deal with if you have time on your side, and your whole life to look forward to. But the death of a friend, a fellow youngster, a person who lived the same lifestyle as you and made your life better for having known them, that is something that even a carefree teenager would find hard to get over. Tragically, over the years since Wigan Casino closed, the Northern Soul scene has lost more than its fair share of its folk, and I have lost more than my fair share of friends.

Penny Fisher, or Fish as we knew her, lived in Kidderminster and was one of the many people from that town who visited the Casino. Penny was, to quote her friends, a complete nut-case: she had an odd sense of humour which would manifest itself unexpectedly when you were in her company. Every time I met her she greeted me with a big hug and her trade mark saying: "Oh my Gawd!!" She had such a sunny outlook on life that it was rare to see her with anything less than a huge grin on her face, a smile that would cheer you up even in your worst mood. Another of her unforgettable features was her booming laugh. I can see her even now, doubled-up with delight at one of her own jokes, and this deep, throaty laughter filling the room until tears appeared behind her glasses and ran down her cheeks. One of the nicest welcomes of an Oldies All-nighter would be when the Wolvo crowd joined-up with the Kidderminster and Redditch coach at junction 10 of the M6; the first person that you would see would be Fish, waving her arms like a pair of windmill blades, laughing loudly and shouting "Oh my Gawd!!"

Privately, Penny was usually hung up with boyfriend trouble, though she never showed the world anything but a smile. One of her closest friends, Elaine, once told me: "Fish always fell in love too fast, and she could never believe that anyone would want to hurt her." Penny died in 1986 following an accidental over-dose of a prescribed drug.

Phil Shelton always gave you the impression that he was one jump ahead of the rest of the world; his broad smile seemed to hide a million secrets, and usually did. Phil was one of our own crowd, and he seemed to know everybody on the scene by their first names. My earliest memory of him was at the Lafayette at one of the weekly soul sessions: I remember him standing near the DJ decks, clutching a record which he was asking the DJ Blue Max to play for him. When Max asked him why, Phil replied: "Because it's f— brilliant, what other reason do you need?" The record was Dutch Robinson's "Can't Get Along Without You", which Phil had bought before it became a dance floor monster, indeed, before anyone else had even heard of it.

Phil seemed to want to put as much into every day as was humanly possible, he was always the one to suggest where to go to the crowd who used to assemble in the Old Vic Hotel each weekend. He always seemed to get the front seat too, next to the driver. The rest of us were crammed into the back of Paul's Datsun Cherry, and Phil would be stretched out in comfort in the front. True, he was a tall lad at about six feet one, but if you knew him as we did, you know that even if he had been five feet one, he would still have found a way of getting the best seat.

Some of my fondest memories of him were not at soul venues at all, but on boozy nights out around the town centre pubs and discos. Phil's prowess with the girls made the rest of us look like monks, but he was just as capable of delivering a killer put-down line to a young lady, as he was of getting her 'phone number for future reference. Sadly, his appetite for excess proved too great once too often.

I was invited to the funerals of both Penny and Phil, but I attended neither. After the grief that followed their deaths, my overwhelming feeling was one of anger. An anger directed at whoever it is that decides that people like Phil and Penny will never have their own families and grow old with their memories. A rage which cannot find a outlet in any material target. What do you do? Do you curse at the sky and hope that someone is listening? But most of all, an anger at the stupid, senseless waste of two lives. Penny and Phil had so much to offer, and their whole lives ahead of them, now they only live in the memories and thoughts of those that loved them. I did not need to go to their funerals to be reminded of that.

I also need to mention the following friends, some close, some no more than acquaintances, who are no longer with us: Bryn Lane and Steve Morris, both from Wolverhampton, Martin Randle from Kingswinford, Pete Lawson from Ormskirk, Mick Vickers from Crewe, Roch from Yate, Mud from Leicester, Alan from Stockport, Ruth from Worcester, and from Wigan – Kenny Spence, Mike Walker and Gerry Marshall. Their names are just groups of letters on a page, but their lives added so much to the lives of the people they left behind.

People have said to me: "I still dream about being there" or, "Not one day goes by when I don't think about the old days", or "Sometimes I wish I'd never gone to the Casino, because then I wouldn't miss it so much". I have had those dreams, too.

Without Wigan Casino, a lot of people had trouble coming to terms with their lives; it was the biggest part of their lives, the one thing that they lived for, and they found it impossible to replace. Marriage and having children takes you into a different world, the world of responsibility and adulthood, and the happiness they bring occupies the biggest part of your life. But family life, vital though it is, does nothing to replace the memory of a phenomenon like Wigan Casino. Time and again in recent years I have bumped into people at soul venues that I have not seen since 1981. Away from the scene for many years, to get married and start a family, sooner or later, they always come back. If you are a true soulie and if the music really has got a hold of you, you will return to it.

Whilst writing this book it has dawned on me that the answer is not to try to forget it, but to remember it without regret. Time is a funny thing; you can't bring back the past, any more than you can live only for the future. All there is, is here and now. Yesterday is gone forever, and tomorrow might never come, so you can only borrow from the past in order to make the present a bit more bearable. Stuff the future, that will never turn out the way you really want it to, how ever hard you plan for it. So, to everybody who lived and breathed Wigan Casino as I did, and who now still yearns to go back there, I have the solution to our problems; when you look back, don't mourn its passing, celebrate its being there in the first place! We have no reason to feel regret, that is for the people who never went. We have no reason for sadness, because WE WERE THERE! We were as much a part of it, as it is still a part of us, and it will stay a part of us for as long as we breathe. Our lives will always be richer for being able to say: "Yes. I went to Wigan Casino."

Keep the faith.

If you enjoyed Dave Shaw's *Casino* you may want to read

The In Crowd

MIKE RITSON & STUART RUSSELL

The Northern Soul scene was exciting, amphetamine-fast and resolutely underground. Spread almost exclusively by word-of-mouth, it managed to avoid the attention of a national press, preoccupied as ever, with events in the capital. *The In Crowd* charts and celebrates the extraordinary story of, what was once, one of the best kept secrets of the early '70s. The first volume begins with the hip R&B collectors, mods and Motown fans who took the Golden Era of '60s Soul as a blueprint for this astonishing culture. The foreword is written by soul journalist Dave Godin, credited with first penning the term Northern Soul.

"Good things come to those who wait, it is said. Well, the Northern Soul scene has certainly been waiting a scandalously long time for a book to do it justice. That oversight has now been corrected. This book is not good, it's awesome."
NEIL RUSHTON *Echoes*

"The In Crowd is a massive piece of work that fills in the gaps left by other books that have set out to document the phenomenon known as Northern Soul. ...It's a fantastic read and the 320 pages are crammed with loads of hair-tingling photos of the old clubs, DJs and artists."
YOGI HAUGHTON *Edinburgh Evening News*

"Eventually the scene imploded, overexposed and under-attended, but this volume testifies to the fascination that it still holds, and not only for the survivors."
STEVE JELBERT *The Times*

"The research is astounding. No record, artist, label or venue too small to be mentioned, no issue too controversial to duck – bootlegging, cash-ins, drugs devastation and resulting club closures...
The In Crowd is perfection. Can't wait for 'Volume 2.'"
LOIS WILSON *Mojo*

£29.95 paperback
ISBN 0 9536626 1 6
www.beecool.co.uk